MILES ON THE MOUNTAIN

SKIING AT SIXTY-FOUR AND OTHER ADVENTURES

MILES ON THE MOUNTAIN

SKIING AT SIXTY-FOUR AND OTHER ADVENTURES

CHARLIE AVERA

LitPrime Solutions
21250 Hawthorne Blvd
Suite 500, Torrance, CA 90503
www.litprime.com
Phone: 1 (209) 788-3500

© 2020 Charlie Avera. All rights reserved.

No part of this book may be reproduced, stored in a retrieval system, or transmitted by any means without the written permission of the author.

Published by LitPrime Solutions   11/25/2020

ISBN: 978-1-953397-37-9(sc)
ISBN: 978-1-953397-38-6(e)

Library of Congress Control Number: 2020923144

Any people depicted in stock imagery provided by Thinkstock are models, and such images are being used for illustrative purposes only.

Certain stock imagery © Thinkstock.

Because of the dynamic nature of the Internet, any web addresses or links contained in this book may have changed since publication and may no longer be valid. The views expressed in this work are solely those of the author and do not necessarily reflect the views of the publisher, and the publisher hereby disclaims any responsibility for them.

CONTENTS

Dedication vii
Preface ix
Acknowledgment xi
Introduction xiii

The First Day: December 31, 2013 1
Doing Time in Michigan 4
Home to Colorado 6
Diagnosis: MS 8
Caregiving 10
A Few Short Trips 13
Hiking 14
Mount Evans: A "14er" 16
Skiing: The Early Days 24
My Homemade Ski Machine 30
Christy Sports Powder Daze 33
Second Year (2014–2015) 34
    Winter Park: Learning to Stop 36
    Winter Park: Cranmer and the ER 37
    Breckenridge: March 2015 40
Third Year (2015–2016) 42
    Skiing with Ravi 44
    Focused Improvement 45
    Left Turn Stopping 46
    Smooth Turns and Speed Control 47
    Increasing My Speed 47

- Fourth Year (2016–2017) 48
  - White Rabbit, Jabberwocky, Cheshire Cat, Mary Jane, and Parsenn Bowl 50
    - White Rabbit 50
    - Jabberwocky 51
    - Cheshire Cat 52
    - Mary Jane 52
    - Parsenn Bowl 54
  - Loveland Ski Area: Paying It Forward 56
  - Loveland Valley: Lift 3 58
  - The Last Day of the Season: March 11 59
  - Ski Patrol 62
  - Season Ending 64
- Taking Inventory and Looking Forward 66
  - It is an Addiction 67
- Epilogue: January 2019 69

DEDICATION

For my brother, John, who lost his long battle with diabetes on June 6, 2017. Although our paths did not often cross in our adult years, he was still a wonderful brother, and I will cherish my fond memories of the years we shared growing up. After years of suffering in a failing body, he now runs freely with the angels.

And for Jeanne, John's loving wife and lifelong soulmate, who was also his faithful caregiver to the end.

PREFACE

For many who call Colorado home and enjoy its tremendous variety of outdoor sports, learning to ski in our beautiful Rocky Mountains is a rite of passage. Each year, thousands of young people start their unique journeys, carefully measuring their improvement with each new ski season.

Miles on the Mountain is the story of my adventures as I began my own skiing journey. But what is different about my story is that when I started skiing, my youth was a very distant memory.

When I first thought about writing this book, I was sixty-two years old and had just finished my second season of skiing in Colorado. I wanted to capture my experiences during these first two years like a diary, carefully recording the events while they were still fresh in my memory. I wanted a simple narrative for my kids and grandkids to enjoy and to become a part of our family story. I wanted this to be a fun, funny, and informative story, telling how and why I took up this fun sport later in life. *Miles on the Mountain* invites you to join me in my skiing adventures, from my very first day at Copper Mountain, progressing through the next four years, season by season.

ACKNOWLEDGMENT

Even though we had lived in Colorado for over twenty years, I did not start skiing until I was sixty. The fun that I now enjoy skiing at Colorado's great resorts I owe to my daughter Beth, who one day, simply asked me if I wanted to go skiing.

At the time, Beth had been in the Air Force for about eight years. She was in the intelligence field, proudly serving to protect our freedoms as an airborne equipment operator and instructor. She had flown over five hundred combat missions while on various deployments in the Middle East, flying over some of the most dangerous parts of the world. But on the slopes, she looks just like any other young snowboarder. You would never guess that she was such a highly skilled airborne warrior.

These four years of skiing have been an incredible adventure for me, and through it all, Beth has been a very patient and helpful coach, and a source of encouragement and motivation. She never let me quit, even when I wanted to.

Thank you, Beth!

INTRODUCTION

To be clear, this is just a story about an old man who started skiing at an older age. I do not do flips, jumps, big air, rails, or other tricks. Compared to what kids do today at the X-Games and Red Bull competitions, my story is lame. But my kids, grandkids, and close friends have been impressed with this old man's achievement, and that is all I am trying to capture with this story.

I was sixty-two years old when I began writing this story. I did not want this story to be boring. As a career computer programmer, I have read and written many technical documents. I know how dry and boring these can be. The very last thing I wanted was to create another technical document about how to start skiing when you are old.

As I began putting my thoughts to the keyboard, more ideas and memories began to flood my mind. Perhaps you might want to know why I waited so long to start skiing. Maybe you are wondering if my life after sixty included other outdoor activities as well.

I have been a caregiver for my wife for over twenty years. I thought perhaps you might want to know what that is like, since it played a large part in my experience.

So, I added some background stories that contributed to my decision to embark on this long-overdue midlife crisis.

By the time I finally captured most of my thoughts from my first two seasons, I was nearly done with my third season, so I added those memories to the story as well. It was an incredibly fun season, and I wanted to remember the experiences accurately while they were still fresh in my mind.

After putting some final touches on the story, and adding lots of pictures, I sent it to the kids, to my brothers and sisters, to a few friends, and to my mom, who lives with my sister in northwest Washington. The response was positive. My brother John called it a novel, although I think it is a little bit short for a novel. However, the responses from him and my mom were interesting and inspiring.

While I only wanted to capture my skiing adventures, my mom had a different take. At ninety years old, and still mentally sharp and physically active, she read a story of encouragement, persistence, and resilience. Mom still hikes near her home with my sister, and she said this story gave her motivation and encouragement to keep going.

My brother, John, had suffered for years from severe diabetes. He was on dialysis due to kidney failure and lost his foot and lower leg to infection, all a result of the diabetes. His wife became his full-time caregiver. He provided some insight into the frustrations of one who receives constant care from another:

> "You talked at some length about being a caregiver for Jan, I know how much pressure I put on Jeanne, every time I want or need something I have to ask Jeanne to take me or go get it. As **INDEPENDENT** as I've always been, it's soooo hard for me to ask for anything. Come August it will have been *2 yrs* since I lost my leg and about *3* since I lost use of it. Jeanne retired about *2* years early to take care of me *&* I can't see how I would have made it without her. The leg I have as a replacement doesn't fit (I can't get it over my knee and my sheen [sic] rubs against the plastic and hurts after about *5* or *6* steps*)* and I too am stuck in this wheelchair, I hate being in this chair*!!!*"

After sending this first draft to everyone, I thought I was done. But after proofreading it several more times, I noticed that it just read like a whole bunch of short headlines strung together to make a very disconnected narrative at best. There was no feeling or emotion in it. It lacked any real sense of adventure. It was like a stick drawing when what I really wanted was a fine painting. It read more like a grocery list or a phonebook than a compelling action story. It was technical and boring, precisely everything I did not want it to be.

So I spent some more time reworking it, developing a fuller story that better captures the excitement and thrill that I enjoyed along this journey, as well as the pain of the falls and injuries I sustained along the way. Not that I was overly excited about falling on the slopes and getting hurt, but that was also a very real part of my experience.

I was much happier with this second draft.

All the events in this story are true to the best of my memory. I have not embellished them, except to try to present them in an interesting, entertaining, and sometimes humorous way. That is my style. Except where noted, all the hiking and skiing pictures are mine, taken from either my phone or frames extracted from my GoPro videos. A few pictures also came from my daughters' cameras.

I hope you enjoy reading about the skiing adventures of an old man desperately trying to stay young and cling to what active years he might have left. That was my original idea. But if this story also encourages you to keep pursuing your dreams when your body is telling you it is time to quit, or you gain some empathy for a worn-out caregiver you may know, then I am truly happy that it has also helped in that regard.

I had a great time writing and refining this over the past few years, and my hope is that you enjoy reading it as much as I enjoyed writing it.

Old age comes at a bad time.
—San Banducci

Live your life and forget your age.
—Norman Vincent Peale

THE FIRST DAY: DECEMBER 31, 2013

Colorado's Copper Mountain is a great ski resort. When you take exit 195 off I-70 at Copper Mountain and drive the short distance to the parking lot, you immediately discover why this is such a popular ski destination. Spread over three mountains, Copper has over 140 trails on nearly 2500 skiable acres. Okay, that is what the brochure says. The first time I saw the slopes and the lifts going nearly straight up from the base, I had a slightly different impression: I was terrified! I had never skied before, and I had absolutely no idea what I was doing. The very idea of speeding down a steep, snow-covered mountain slope on a pair of skinny sticks with no seatbelts or airbags or any other safety equipment flew in the face of all the common sense that six decades of life experiences had taught me.

But my daughter, Beth, an avid and very experienced snowboarder, was home for Christmas and wanted to spend a day on the slopes. Having no one to go with, she asked me if I wanted to try skiing. Really? I was almost sixty-one years old, and I had never been on a pair of skis. I have lived this long because I stopped doing dangerous things a long time ago. All I have heard about old guys skiing is that they all have heart attacks or run into trees. So, in my opinion, I had good reason to stay safe at home and live a few more years.

But she was persistent, and I had no intention of letting her know how scared I really was. Besides, it would be some special quality time with my young warrior. As an airborne intelligence equipment operator in the Air Force, she was deployed to several hot spots in the Middle East and had flown hundreds of missions over many other dangerous places. How could I turn her down? So on the last day of 2013, with rental skis, boots, poles, and helmet thrown in the back of the Blazer and my last will and testament updated, we were on our way up I-70 to Copper Mountain, wherever that was.

Colorado's Rocky Mountains are home to many great ski areas and resorts. We live just southwest of Denver between Littleton and Morrison in unincorporated Jefferson County, at the base of the foothills and about two miles south of the famous Red Rocks Amphitheater. From there, it is about an hour's drive to Loveland Ski Area and Winter Park Ski Resort. Copper Mountain, Breckenridge, and Arapahoe Basin are about a half hour farther. It is very convenient to drive up to one of these areas, spend a day on the slopes, and be back home in time for dinner.

On this first day, I was lost in my thoughts as we drove up to Copper Mountain. *Would I enjoy this, or would it be a disaster?* I did not say much, and Beth probably sensed that I was really nervous. Going through the Eisenhower Tunnel far beneath the Continental Divide was a metaphor for me, with images of that bright light at the end of the tunnel. After passing through the tunnel, we had about eighteen miles to go until we reached Copper Mountain. That was eighteen miles to reflect on my life.

We reached the resort and finally found a parking lot. We did not know there was free parking with a shuttle service, so we ended up paying twenty-five dollars to park close to the center village. After we parked, I started looking around the parking lot to see what everyone else was doing. I have learned that if you do not know what you are doing, just copy what others around you are doing, act confident, and fake it. Most of the time, it works.

I noticed everyone was busy putting on their ski boots, hats, helmets, goggles, and coats, and gathering their equipment. They all looked like they knew what they were doing and were going to have a lot of fun. I tried to do what they were doing. But I did not get everything right on this first day.

I was so new to this sport that I did not even know how to properly wear my thermals. There in the parking lot, I dutifully tucked my long johns deep into my ski boots. I will explain later why this turned out to be a really bad thing. But at this early stage in my budding ski career, I just did not know any better. All I knew was that I was nervous and scared, but I certainly did not want to tarnish my macho mystique.

From the parking lot, we made our way to the village, where I signed up for their never-done-this-before beginner ski lesson package. As I was explaining to the lady behind the counter that I had never skied before, she took one look at me, probably trying to guess how old I was, and asked if I wanted to do the tubing hill instead. *Really? Did I really look that old and frail?* I think most people who sign up for these beginner classes are either little kids or young adults. I bet she did not see very many sixty-year-olds signing up for the beginner class. I may have been nervous and scared, but Beth and I were determined to get me skiing today. I was not interested in the tubing hill. I went ahead and signed up for the beginner course.

We stopped for a cup of coffee before heading out to the slopes. Looking up at sheer vertical slopes from the cafeteria only exacerbated those not-so-warm-and-fuzzy feelings I had been experiencing up to this point.

And so, the first day of my skiing career was about to launch. On to the bunny hill. Move over kids, here comes Grandpa.

It is not uncommon to see older skiers on the slopes. After all, seventy is the new fifty, right? I have talked to lots of skiers who were fifty, sixty, or even older. And on any given day, you will see lots of folks who are skiing for the first time in their lives. Most of them are fearless little kids who do not know they are supposed to be scared, or young adults practicing various methods of falling down the mountain. I have the greatest respect for new skiers. But after four years of skiing, I do not recall seeing any old people learning to ski for the first time.

So, it is not very common to see an old man sharing the bunny hill with a bunch of little kids, trying to ski for the first time. It was awkward, and I suspect that I looked quite silly. I was way out of my comfort zone—watching kids gliding smoothly down the little bunny hill, while I spent as much time on the ground as I did upright. I now know what they mean when they talk about hitting the slopes.

Although this was my first day on a pair of skis, my skiing adventure actually had its roots over twenty years earlier.

All right, then, I'll go to hell.
—Mark Twain

DOING TIME IN MICHIGAN

Before moving to Colorado in 1992, we lived in Michigan. No, we did seven years in Michigan. Coming from South Carolina, I found that living in Michigan was like living in a different country. In 1986, after graduating from the University of South Carolina with a business degree, I went to work for Electronic Data Systems. GM had bought the company two years before, and nearly everyone they hired was immediately sent off to the rust belt. The only requirements they had for their new recruits were that they had a pulse and a college degree. I met these minimum requirements, so in January of 1986, we left Greenville, SC, and moved to Michigan.

If you love Michigan and are easily offended when someone speaks unkindly about your beloved state, then you should skip the next few paragraphs and perhaps take this opportunity to make an appointment to get some help. Seriously. I did not grow up in Michigan, I have no emotional attachment to the state, and about the only fond memory I have of the years we lived there is when we packed up the U-Haul and moved to Colorado.

Where did we live in Michigan? Michigan looks a little bit like the palm of your right hand, so when someone asks where you live, you just hold up your hand and point. If you live anywhere near Grand Rapids, you point to the heel of your hand. If you live near Lansing, the state capital, then you point to the middle of your palm, and if you live near Detroit, like we did, you point to the bottom of your thumb. We lived under the thumb for seven long years.

And nearly everyone who lives around Detroit works directly or indirectly for one of the big three automakers: GM, Ford, or Chrysler. Since GM owned EDS, I worked on a GM account. First in one of the assembly plants, and then developing diagnostic software.

The UAW and other unions have a huge influence in that part of the country—both on and off the job—by convincing low-information workers to trade their common sense for union cards. When I worked in the assembly plant, the union workers made about eighteen dollars an hour plus overtime. Not much after years of working in a factory. But at least they got to sleep on the job.

It was no secret at work that after about a year, I did not like living in Michigan. One of my GM counterparts, and a native Michigander, once told me that I needed to drive about a hundred miles north to enjoy the state. Really? After living in Colorado for twenty years, I still enjoy just walking across the street to get my mail. I cannot imagine living in a place where I have to drive two hours away to enjoy it.

I soon discovered that In Michigan, there are only two seasons and one pastime: cold, gray winters and drinking beer, followed by hot, gray summers and drinking beer. Everywhere I went, everyone seemed to sport big beer-bellies, both men and women. When the women went shopping in the spring after a long cold gray winter drinking lots of beer, I thought they just did not know what they looked like. There is nothing as gross as a fat lady blocking the aisle at the local Meijers store dressed in shorts and a halter top. If they knew what they looked like, they would never go outside. I had to wonder if any of them had any mirrors in their homes. But I guess that is just how they live in Michigan.

© *Photo by pabradyphoto, royalty-free image from istockphoto.com*
<https://www.istockphoto.com/photo/welcome-to-colorful-colorado-gm656836002-119628945>

Go west, young man.
—Horace Greeley

HOME TO COLORADO

So, after doing seven hard years in Michigan, I was more than ready for a change. I put in a request for a transfer, and in November 1992 we packed all our stuff in a U-Haul and moved to Colorado. This was the best move we ever made and the start of an adventure that I have never regretted.

The best memory I have of Michigan is seeing the state sign getting smaller and smaller in the rearview mirror.

We have now lived in Colorado for twenty-one years; twice as long as anywhere else we ever lived.

The beauty and grandeur of the Rocky Mountains never grows old. Hiking in the foothills near our home is always an awesome adventure. Driving to work down C-470 in the early morning often provides a grand view of Pikes Peak, sixty miles in the distance. And driving home in the afternoon, the Rockies majestically stretch to the north and south as far as you can see, as if you can just reach out and touch them.

It is in this setting that we settled and raised our family for the next twenty years.

We fell in love with Colorado right from the start, and after about six months, we were able to buy the house we still live in today. Our house is in unincorporated Jefferson County, about twenty miles southwest of Denver, nestled just east of the foothills at the base of the Rocky Mountains. Ours is a quiet and friendly neighborhood. Looking north down our street, we have a grand view of Green Mountain, one of many foothills near our house. After two decades, we still love it as much as we did when we first moved in. I do not think it will ever get old.

But with six children, it was certainly not easy. Anyone who has raised a family knows how challenging it can be, no matter where you live. Money was always tight, and there was never enough to take up expensive hobbies. So even though we lived next to the Rocky Mountains, home of the greatest skiing in the country, I rarely thought about taking up the sport. With eight of us, it would cost thousands to enjoy a season of family skiing. There was always too much month left over at the end of each paycheck.

But those first few years in Colorado were not nearly as challenging as what was in store for us in the years to come.

DIAGNOSIS: MS

In 1994, my wife, Jan, began having problems with her balance, and she was also experiencing some numbness in her legs. We told ourselves it was probably just a pinched nerve or something. Give it time, and it would go away. But it did not go away. In fact, as the weeks wore on, her condition only got worse. Her balance was nearly gone, and she could barely walk. The doctors could not pinpoint any specific cause, but I later found out that our primary care doctor suspected early on that it might be multiple sclerosis, or MS. He was wise to not tell us his suspicions until a diagnosis could be confirmed. That confirmation came in May 1995.

By October of 1995, she was in a wheelchair, unable to walk unassisted, and she has not walked on her own since. After another exacerbation in December, she spent a month in the Spaulding Rehabilitation Hospital here in Denver. In our ignorance, we thought this stay would help her get back to normal. Instead, it was really to teach her how to function with her new limitations. Over the next two decades, she would have more stays in hospitals and rehabilitation centers because of more exacerbations, infections, and even a serious bout with sepsis, a life-threatening infection in the blood. She would endure countless PT sessions, OT sessions, and who knows how many in-home nurse visits. She would also break her ankles four different times (three times within two weeks, requiring surgery), crush her big toe, and break two bones in her foot, all directly related to the debilitating effects of her MS.

Visiting Mom in Kansas, April 2003

Multiple sclerosis is a neurological disorder that affects different people in different ways. Some people can continue to live fairly normal lives, for some time. For others, it is more devastating. For everyone, it changes everything. By December of 1996, Jan had suffered several more exacerbations and soon was barely able to move at all. At one point, she could not even lift a fork to feed herself. We did not know what the future had in store for us. We were naive and still believed this would go away in time. But the MS never went away, and every day, every week, every month, every year introduced new challenges. We were constantly redefining what was normal for us.

For the next fifteen years, my life was consumed with taking care of Jan, raising the family, and working. There was not much time and certainly no money left over to take up expensive hobbies. Even if I could afford to take up skiing, it would have to wait. I was always focused on managing the problems each day brought our way. Let me give you a glimpse into my world of caregiving.

*Sometimes, I need to go off on my own. I'm not sad.
I'm not angry. I'm just recharging my batteries.*
—Anonymous

CAREGIVING

N<small>O ONE THINKS ABOUT BEING</small> a caregiver until the responsibility is thrust upon them. Then it is baptism by fire, on-the-job training, learn as you go. Everyone who becomes a caregiver has a unique situation that only they can learn and adjust to over time.

When we were thrust into this, I did not find any useful guides for caregivers. No *Caregiving for Dummies 101*. And information from online caregiver sites was so general that it proved to be little help to me. I could not find any effective caregiver support groups. If there were support groups for our situation, they were one of healthcare's best-kept secrets. After a few years I just quit looking. We had to feel our way through this mostly on our own. On the upside, physical therapists were helpful. But the occupational therapists who came to the house just seemed to keep telling us that we needed to spend thousands of dollars to transform our house into a little hospital ward. I grew weary of that too and learned to just figure out what I needed by myself. I think that caregivers eventually realize that they are mostly on their own.

I can only speak from my own experience after twenty years of caring for Jan, and I will speak in that context. But there are also many wives who dutifully care for their husbands, parents who care for their children, and children who care for their parents. I can only speak of caring for Jan, who has been wheelchair-bound for twenty years now, because that is what I know.

Because of her MS, Jan faces physical, mental, and emotional challenges every day. That is what we are supposed to say to be politically correct. But I have no use for political correctness and all the silly verbal gyrations and contortions that go along with that foolishness, so I just say she is handicapped. She is not offended by that. It means the same thing and is a lot easier to spell and type. And besides, we get to park in the handicapped parking spaces.

When Jan was first diagnosed with MS, and we were beginning to feel our way around this caregiver thing, I discovered a lot about myself as well as other people. I soon learned that while most people will often express a concern for her and ask how she's doing, they really don't want to be bothered with details. It did not take long to learn to politely smile and say, "She's doing okay." But I found that I could be more open and franker with family; they genuinely cared and always wanted to know more about her condition. While they could do little to help because they all live out of state, just knowing that they cared more than most provided comfort and encouragement.

It is not a matter of resentment or bitterness, either. I think all caregivers come to this realization early in their experience; it is human nature. People have their own lives to live, and I would never expect anyone to take on my responsibilities. Not even my kids.

Caregivers live in their own, private world. They quietly go about providing the care their loved one needs. Few will ever know how many hours we will give in our lifetime. Few caregivers will ever be recognized for the selfless work we do because we are not first responders; we are all-the-time responders. I work my full-time job and then come home to take care of Jan, helping her do those things she cannot do by herself. Others certainly have it worse than I do, but my responsibilities take on the nature of a second job. I do all the shopping, laundry, yard work, home maintenance, and much of the housework. I also manage the finances, taxes, insurance, and other business of our household. When that is done, or sometimes postponed or ignored, I help her with personal matters that she can no longer do by herself. And when she has a doctor or dentist appointment, I must take time off work and take her. These are some of the things that caregivers just do. And I do it on a single income.

I decided early that, for me, it would just not be right to go off and have fun with friends while Jan was home stuck in a wheelchair. So, for over fifteen years, I seldom did anything other than work and caregiving. I went to a few Rockies ballgames with my son and justified it because it was spending quality time with family. But I did not do other activities that I might normally do just for me. Hiking, camping, and hunting come to mind. Golf does not.

You cannot spot a caregiver in a crowd unless they are pushing a wheelchair or helping their loved one. They are the quiet heroes of our society, always giving and seldom asking for anything in return. And they are always tired and worn out. I know, because after about fifteen years I too was getting tired and worn out. But quitting is not an option, so we just keep being the caregivers, tired and worn out.

But eventually, I began to reconsider my ideas about not doing anything for myself. Jan had demonstrated that she could manage sufficiently on her own and could be at home safely for most of the day. After all, I still had to go to work each day, and we have contingencies if anything serious happens while I am away. Cell phones came on the scene at just the right time, and 911 is our ultimate contingency plan. Let me tell you a funny story about one 911 call we made.

Of course, there is nothing funny about a 911 call, but let me explain. One day, Jan was suddenly having much more difficulty standing up and transferring to her wheelchair than she normally did. She was lethargic, almost like she had been drugged. We had experienced this once before, and that time the problem turned out to be a serious infection. Today she fell while transferring to her wheelchair, ending up on the floor. I could not get her back into her wheelchair by myself, so I called 911.

West Metro Fire Department here in Jefferson County has a policy that if they do not transfer a patient to the hospital, then there is no charge for the 911 call. I was taking no chances, and I needed to get her to the ER. But I knew if I could just get her into our Blazer, then I would be able to get her to the hospital with no problem. I had done it several times before, and it would save the cost of an ambulance ride.

The paramedics and firemen were able to get her into her wheelchair and out to the Blazer without any problem. On a good day it is only a little bit of a challenge for her to transfer from the wheelchair to the front seat of the Blazer. When she can stand by herself at the open door, it is not too hard. She sits down in the front seat and I pick her legs up and swing her in. But today, I knew it would be more difficult. I got her into position to do the transfer, with one of the responders holding the door open. While I was helping her transfer, the responder looked at me and, with a straight face, said, "Do you want us to take this door off for you? We can do that, you know." We all had a good laugh and I got her to the hospital just fine, with the Blazer door still intact.

We have had to make several 911 calls over the years. A few times Jan was transported to the hospital. It turned out that these trips were fully covered by our insurance after all. Then there were other times where they only had to help her get back into her wheelchair because she had fallen. But since these calls have been infrequent, I felt more at ease leaving her alone at home when it was necessary. My real concern was if I had to be away for more than a day or two. My job has never required any overnight travel, but sometimes I had the opportunity to attend some special events that required me to be away for a few days each time.

A FEW SHORT TRIPS

A FEW TIMES OVER THE YEARS, I have been able take some short trips lasting a few days for some special occasions. When my oldest son, Joshua, graduated from his Air Force Basic Military Training in 1999, I went to San Antonio for the ceremony and spent a few days with him. Of course, this was only four years after Jan was diagnosed with MS, and she was not as limited as she is today. Then when my dad passed away in 2003, I was able to go to Arizona for his memorial service. And again, when my mom needed help fixing the house before selling it, I flew down to Phoenix. My brother, John, picked me up at the airport and we drove a hundred miles up to Clarkdale. I inherited a few of my mom's things that I brought back to Colorado in a U-Haul. It was a long drive home, and the whole trip kept me away for a few days. Thankfully, Jan had no significant problems while I was gone.

After Beth finished some special training for her top-secret Air Force job, I was able to spend a few days at her graduation at Goodfellow AFB in San Angelo, Texas. And when she graduated from Airman Leadership School a few years later, I had the privilege of attending that ceremony at Hurlburt Field, just west of Fort Walton Beach on Florida's panhandle.

So, after about fifteen years, I began thinking that perhaps she did not need my caregiving skills around the clock. I thought just maybe, after all these years, it would be okay to take a break and enjoy doing some things for myself without feeling guilty.

So, in September 2011, when my oldest daughter, Becky, asked me if I wanted to go on a hike in the hills just west of Golden, I said, "Let's do it." It had been years since I had done anything like that, an activity, just for me.

Fill your life with experiences, not things. Have stories to tell, not stuff to show.
—Anonymous

HIKING

It is not like hiking would become an obsession with me. After all, I was getting up in years, and after many years of relative inactivity, I was not in the best physical shape. So, to launch out on a four-mile hike might be a challenge. And remember, this was in the foothills of the Rocky Mountains at an elevation of seven thousand feet or more, with steep inclines and elevation gains. I had not done any strenuous exercise in years. And there are rattlesnakes in those hills. As Indiana Jones said it so well, "I hate snakes." To me, it was the perfect recipe for a heart attack.

Over the years, ranchers and landowners in many Colorado counties have graciously donated their land to be designated as public open space. These areas are great for hiking, horseback riding, running, biking, and sometimes camping. Most of these open spaces prohibit motorcycles and ATVs, and the county works hard to preserve the natural beauty of the area. On the trails, people are very friendly, and the views are simply breathtaking.

But hiking in our foothills is not easy. At least not for me. As I get older, the strain on my back and hips on a four- or five-mile hike takes its toll. When I finish one of these hikes, I am usually pretty worn out, stiff, and sore, even for a day or two after the hike. But the reward is in the beauty of our hills, and the views along the way or at the top. There is also the gratification of accomplishing a difficult feat. Each hike is an adventure of its own; some are difficult, while others are easier. But every hike I have been on has been rewarding.

Our first hike was at White Ranch Open Space, an area a few miles off Highway 93, just west of Golden in Jefferson County. White Ranch Open Space has several trails and a campground. The trail we followed that day was a 4.5-mile loop. Part of the trail is open meadows, and part is tree-covered. Some parts are gentle slopes, and some are steep ravines. All of it is stunning. White Ranch is probably my favorite open space hiking area. For a first hike, it was nothing short of a home run. And even though it is relatively close to Golden, it still feels far removed from the daily grind. Over the years, we have hiked many other trails, including Mount Falcon, Dawson's Butte, and Roxborough State Park, but White Ranch will always be special.

Looking north in Roxborough State Park

Mountains have a way of dealing with overconfidence.
—John Muir

Zombies eat brains. You're safe.
—The Fresh Quotes

MOUNT EVANS: A "14ER"

Colorado has fifty-two peaks in the Rocky Mountains whose summits are over fourteen thousand feet in elevation. For many Colorado hikers, conquering one or more of these "14ers" is a truly rewarding experience as well as providing bragging rights.

In July 2012, Beth was home on leave, and Becky asked us if we wanted to do a 14er. Mount Bierstadt is reportedly the easiest peak to climb, with a scenic 3.5-mile trail to reach the summit at 14,065 feet and an elevation gain of 2,850 feet. This was what we had planned to hike, but the GPS lady had a different idea for us today. Instead of directing us to Mount Bierstadt, she guided us up Mount Evans Road to Summit Lake, at the base of Mount Evans. Determined to do a 14er, we quickly adjusted our plan and decided to summit Mount Evans at 14,264 feet. To keep this in perspective, pilots are required to use oxygen above ten thousand feet.

The trail to the top of Mount Evans from Summit Lake is not much of a trail at all. We were guided by special stone markers called cairns, a small cluster of four or five rocks neatly stacked one on top of the other. It is like a game, looking for the next stack of rocks, because at this elevation, high above the tree line, there is no clearly defined path or trail. Just rocks. Climbing between 12,830 and 14,264 feet over the relatively short distance of three and a half miles proved to be very demanding at my age and physical condition.

About two miles up the trail, we stopped to take pictures of the Chicago Lakes in the valley a thousand feet below before continuing toward the summit. Two years later, I would do a ten-mile out-and-back hike up that valley floor to these same Chicago Lakes with a group of friends from work. But today, my daughters and I would gaze down on the lakes a thousand feet below from the edge of the steep cliffs. The view was beyond description, and our pictures do it little justice.

Looking down on Chicago Lakes a thousand feet below

Looking up at the Mount Evans trail from Upper Chicago Lake

A little bit beyond the ridge overlooking the Chicago Lakes, we experienced some dangerous weather, which is quite common for the Rocky Mountain peaks above the tree line. In Denver, it was nearly a hundred degrees, but on the mountain, it was only around forty degrees. The wind was strong and gusty, and we experienced some driving rain, sleet, and even light snow.

Lightning is always a threat in the afternoons, and sometimes people are killed by lightning strikes while hiking in our mountains. So, when my daughters noticed that their hair was standing straight out from under their hoodies, we knew we were in trouble. I did not have to worry about my hair standing straight out, because I do not have any. We had to hunker down among some large boulders to wait for a distant lightning storm to pass by. It was all the protection we could find at this altitude.

To reach the summit of Mount Evans on this route, we would first pass over the summit of Mount Spaulding, at 13,842 feet. From Mount Spaulding, we looked up across a huge plateau sloping steeply uphill.

To the right of the plateau is Mount Bierstadt. Maybe this is the path the GPS lady wanted us to follow. But we now had our sights set on Mount Evans, which was now just a little over a mile away. But that mile was a difficult uphill half-mile hike across the plateau at fourteen thousand feet, followed by another half-mile across a rugged ridgeline, where two very steep ridges converge far above Summit Lake to the northeast and Abyss Lake to the southwest. The path along the ridgeline was a few hundred feet below the top of the ridge, cutting and winding its way through thousands of massive granite boulders, looking down on Abyss Lake far below.

After crossing the ridgeline, the trail became a little bit easier, and the sun returned, to our pleasant surprise. We followed the path around a gentle bend and discovered what we should have known already—that Mount Evans, home of the famous Mount Evans Observatory, is also a popular tourist attraction. Mount Evans Road, the same road that took us to the Summit Lake parking lot, ends at the large parking lot at the summit and the observatory.

As we rounded the bend, we saw the parking lot full of cars and tourists. Nice, clean tourists in their casual slacks and bright, short-sleeved shirts. Tourists who simply walked two hundred feet from their cars to the summit and probably bragged about doing a 14er. We were tired, sweaty, and dirty. We had just hiked three miles up a very rugged trail to reach the summit. Did we feel out of place? Nah. This is Colorado, and this was our first 14er.

But the day did not end there. While everyone else had to merely walk across the parking lot to their cars and drive back down Mount Evans Road, my Blazer was still in the Summit Lake parking lot two thousand feet below and several miles away. We could actually see the Blazer through my binoculars, which was a tiny blue speck far below us.

Looking down on Summit Lake from the top of Mount Evans. Our Blazer is somewhere in the small parking lot just to the right of the lake.

Considering the weather and how tired we were, and how rugged the path was the way we had come, we decided to take the road, with all its switchbacks, back down. Maybe someone would have pity on us and give us a ride, but that was not to be. So we hiked nearly five miles back down, crossing some open, barren fields to shorten the distance of the switchbacks on the road, encountered some herds of mountain goats, and finally, a couple hours later, made it back to the Blazer. Beth and Becky were tired, but I was exhausted. But we could proudly say that we, too, had conquered our first 14er.

Having completed my first 14er, I will say I am not a huge fan of them. Not to take anything away from anyone who has summited one or more of them. Those who do have earned my respect, for sure. But there is now little that is compelling me to do more 14ers. At my age, I have nothing to prove. I have the pictures to prove that I have been there and done that.

My guess is that people are not thinking, "I'm impressed. At your age, look what you accomplished." I will bet they are really thinking, *At your age, what in the world were you thinking?* Beyond that,

Who is that old, overweight man dressed in my clothes?

once you are above the tree line, which is around twelve thousand feet, the landscape is barren, like the moon, or Kansas, without any trees. One picture captures it all. Just rocks and short, scrubby vegetation. Everywhere. And a few mountain goats. After a while, it all looks the same. Up close, off in the distance; just like Kansas, it is all the same. Now I know why all the tourists just drove to the top. But I can now say I have hiked one of Colorado's 14ers.

For the next few days, I was very sore, and the back of my legs were badly sunburned. And this hike brought something else to my attention: I was seriously out of shape. I thought I was active and in fairly good shape, but when hiking with a group, they take lots of group pictures. And in our group shots, this old, overweight man kept showing up in our pictures. If he were not wearing my clothes, I would not recognize him. But it *was* me, and I did not like what I saw. As a result of this hike, I began to get serious about my health.

This hike was an all-day event, and Jan had no problems or emergencies while staying home. Of course, Becky had brought her daughters over, so Jan enjoyed the day with the grandkids. And I was becoming more comfortable doing more things just for me.

For three months after Mount Evans, I was really active in a regular exercise regimen. That is, until I tore my rotator cuff. I do not know exactly when I did it, or how, but by September I could barely lift or hold anything extended with my right arm. I could only sleep for about three or four hours before the pain would wake me up at night. As a result, I was always tired at work. Something had to change, so I went to see an orthopedic surgeon. After Dr. Fuller saw my MRI, we scheduled surgery in September of 2012. I had the rotator cuff surgery that so many others have had. This surgery repairs the damage in the shoulder but takes a year to fully recover and requires extensive physical therapy.

This interrupted my new exercise regimen, but only for a short time. After about two weeks, I started walking and riding my spinning bike. Dr. Fuller was concerned that I was pushing my recovery too fast. I was. The therapy plan for this surgery identified certain types of exercises I could do after a certain amount of time. A friend of mine suggested that I start swimming. According to the recovery schedule, swimming was allowed at the nine-month mark. Do not tell my doctor, but I started swimming at seven.

I am not a naturally gifted swimmer, but as a kid, I felt at home in a pool. But when I started swimming after my surgery, I had not been in a pool for over thirty years. In my mind, I could still swim like a fish. But now at sixty, I could barely make it to the other end of the pool. Out of breath, no stamina or rhythm, stopping at each end of the pool to catch my breath, I felt like a big lumbering football lineman. Dick Butkus of Chicago Bears fame, or William "the Refrigerator" Perry come to mind. You might not recognize these names because they are from a different generation. But I am guessing they were not very graceful swimmers.

When I started swimming, I could only do ten laps, and that took me an hour. But I kept at it and after a while I got to where I could swim a mile twice a week. If you do the math, that is thirty-three laps in a twenty-five-meter pool. I still felt like a big lumbering football lineman, and I knew I was usually the slowest swimmer in the pool, but I could do a mile in an hour. It is a great cardio and upper body workout.

By nine or ten months, there was little I could not do, and the shoulder pain that I had was now a distant memory. My exercise regimen was back on track.

By now, I had changed my mind-set about not doing activities for myself. I still took my caregiving responsibilities seriously, but now I would often spend a day enjoying outdoor activities for my sanity and exercise regularly for my health.

Even if you fall on your face, you're still moving forward
—Victor Kiam

SKIING: THE EARLY DAYS

That brings me to December 31, 2013, and the first day of my new skiing career. By all accounts, my first day skiing should have been my last. I spent the morning on the bunny hill, waiting for my beginner ski lesson to start. The bunny hill at Copper Mountain is about a hundred feet from the top to the bottom, with a very gentle slope, and usually full of little kids, some watchful parents, and maybe a couple of ski instructors. Today, add one old grandpa.

Since I had never been on a pair of skis before, I had no idea what to expect as I began gliding across the snow. I had never been on skates or Rollerblades, and the last time I had been on a skateboard was as a ten-year-old kid over fifty years earlier. So, I could not relate to riding on something that was moving along the ground. I had no balance and every time I tried to turn, I would fall. And even when I was not turning, I would fall. When I stopped, I fell. I think I fell a few times just standing there! Moms would make sure their little kids stayed clear of me. I thought this is not really a winter sport; it is a "fall" sport.

When I went for my lesson, the instructor was a seventy-four-year-old lady from the old country who had been skiing since she was two. For real, no kidding. She told us so. How could someone like that relate to an old man who has never skied before? She gave it her best, but I did not get much from this first lesson, and honestly, I was glad when it was over. What I remember most about that first lesson was that I was the guy who still could not turn or stop and was always falling. But by the end of the day, I was at least going down a bigger hill and had graduated from the little kid's bunny hill.

This first day of skiing was memorable, to say the least, but not necessarily in a good way. And it did not end when the skis came off at the end of the day. It was a long walk back to the Blazer, especially in stiff ski boots, lugging my skis and poles as well. And to make matters worse, we forgot where we had parked. We may have walked for another hour through all the condo parking lots before we finally found the Blazer.

Remember when I said that tucking my long johns into my boots was not a good thing? Well, here is the rest of that story.

By the time we finally made it back to the Blazer, my shins were really hurting. When I took my ski boots off, I could see why they hurt so much. Tucking my thermals into my boots caused them to rub my shins raw. Seriously. It was not just a simple irritating blister. My thermal underwear and heavy wool socks had rubbed through the top layer of skin, opening a gaping hole in my right shin. The same thing happened on my left leg, but just not as bad. This cost me eight visits to the Wound Care Center at Porter Hospital. What a way to start my skiing career! It would be nearly two months before I could go skiing again, enough time to carefully reconsider this new sport and decide whether there would even be a next time.

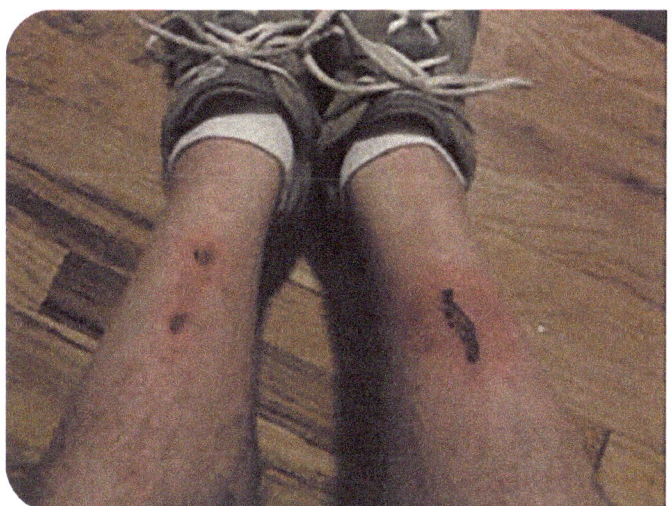 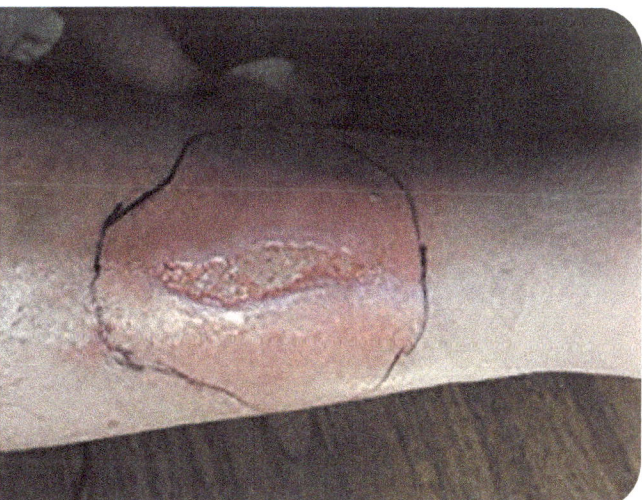

Driving home that day, I had a lot to reflect on. Although Beth and I were able to spend some time together, I really did not enjoy myself at all. And for an experienced snowboarder, it must have been an incredibly boring and even embarrassing day for her. I knew what a failure my first day had been, and I did not want to go again. Okay, I tried it for Beth's sake. Was that not enough?

But then something strange happened. Over the next few days and weeks, I seemed to forget many of the bad things that happened on that first day and thought that maybe I *could* do this. After a few weeks and some encouragement from Beth, I was willing to give it another try at least.

So, in February, after my shins healed enough, we went to Loveland Ski Area to give it another try. Loveland is about an hour up I-70 from our house, at the Continental Divide. The exit for Loveland is just before the Eisenhower Tunnel at Highway 6, where some ski runs come down the mountain high above the tunnel.

Loveland Ski Area is divided into two main sections. The Loveland Valley is where the ski schools and team training areas are located. A mile farther up the frontage road is the main ski area, Loveland Basin, with access to the long green, blue, and black diamond runs.

For those who do not know, ski runs are universally graded by their relative difficulty. Each ski resort usually maintains consistent grading within the resort and grading seems consistent among the different resorts across the country. Each ski trail is identified by both a color and a shape: green circles, blue squares, and black diamonds.

Greens are the easiest runs and are great for beginners. The more difficult trails eventually become green runs as they approach the base of the mountain or the ski lifts and gondolas. Experienced skiers are usually bored with green runs. But you must use them to get back to the ski lifts, when you want to break for lunch, or when you are done for the day.

Blue runs are more difficult and are extremely popular with intermediate skiers. Blues are steeper and faster than greens. When you become an intermediate skier and gain experience and confidence, you look forward to going down more blue runs. Blues are always fun.

Black runs, or as most skiers call them, black diamonds, are much more difficult than blue runs. I do not know why everyone calls them black diamonds, because no one says, "green circles", or "blue squares". But everyone calls them, "black diamonds". Black diamonds are steeper, longer, often covered with moguls (small snow mounds), and may have trees, rocks, sharp turns or other challenging obstacles. Black diamonds are really for intermediate or advanced skiers only. When beginners find themselves on black diamonds, they are noticeably scared and use an abundance of caution to get to the bottom. They also often get in the way of experienced skiers.

Then there are double-black diamonds. Double-black diamonds are extremely difficult and dangerous. They are everything that black diamonds are, but are usually much steeper, not groomed, much longer, and will make even experienced skiers tremble with fear. They usually have "Expert only" signs posted at the top of the run. Double-black diamonds are often located at the very top of the mountain, where suicidal skiers brave extreme conditions to jump onto the vertical walls of the highest mountain bowls, hoping to survive the ride back to the base of the mountain, where there is once again sufficient oxygen to support carbon life forms.

But back to the story. This was still early in my first year. I think I signed up for another lesson or two at Loveland Valley over the next few weeks. I would recommend the ski school for any novice skier. Soon I could go down the short green training hill with ease; I was making progress. Not exactly Olympic material yet, but for me, progress. You can learn ski technique with lessons but gaining confidence and overcoming fear only comes with repetition and experience.

I ended up going to Loveland several more times that first year and soon moved up the road from the Valley to skiing at the Basin. I spent the remainder of that first year going down the two-mile runs from Fire Bowl off Lift 2.

Learning to ski on a safe and gentle training hill is one thing. It is easier when you learn at a young age, but older folks can certainly learn as well. Gravity makes it easy to go downhill and picking up speed is no problem. But turning and controlling your speed is another thing altogether, which takes quite a bit more skill. Stopping was a challenge for me. Using trees and little kids can certainly do the job but are not very practical. Falling was another effective stopping method, but as I began going faster down the hill, falling as a method of stopping became less attractive. It would be a while before I really learned the skill of the "hockey" stop. Until then, I learned to just turn up hill and hope I did not run out of real estate before stopping. And that did not always happen.

So here I was, an absolute beginner skier, going down some gentle two-mile green runs, with extremely limited turning skills and not able to stop if I had to. But I was having fun, and for an old man, it was quite an exciting rush (that is code-speak for scary). The only way to learn how to ski is by skiing, so at the end of each run, I would tell myself how fun it was and say, "Let's do that again."

The beginner's hill was always well-groomed and smooth. The runs at the Basin are groomed as well, but by mid-morning, with all the intermediate and advanced ski traffic, they become rough and bumpy. I still remember the first time I took off down the Fire Bowl, picking up speed, losing control, and hitting my first bumpy patch. It was like driving down a washboard dirt road with no brakes, at least for a few hundred feet. I found a new way to fall. It seems I often had problems with balance whenever I hit these bumpy areas. And since by mid-morning the runs were usually rough and bumpy all the way down, I was struggling to make it all the way without falling. This always rattled my confidence during my first year.

By mid-April of that first year, I had convinced myself that I could do this ski thing after all. It was fun, and I could usually manage to get down to the bottom of each run. My confidence was growing. But someone should have reminded me that I was still a beginner.

On April 16, I wanted to go back to Loveland, but no one else could go with me. So, I decided to go by myself. This is generally not a good idea, for several reasons, especially in your first year. First, skiing is a social sport. It is much more fun to go with family and friends. And second, it is safer to ski with friends. If you get injured, they can help get medical attention, and they can drive you home if you get hurt and cannot drive yourself. In these early years, I often said, "If I can drive home, it was a good day skiing."

Toward the end of each ski season, as the days become warmer, the snow conditions begin to change. The snow melts some during the day and then freezes again at night. So, the early morning runs often have icy patches, and the snow in the afternoon runs begins to be mushy. On this day, I experienced these treacherous conditions firsthand. My first run was okay. I made it down Fire Bowl to one of the Turtle Creek runs and on to the bottom. I hit some icy patches but made it down okay. I told myself, "That was fun. Let's do it again!" So, I did.

On the next run, I had just left Fire Bowl and was going down South Turtle Creek again, when I hit another icy patch. This time, I lost control and took a bad spill. I heard and felt a loud pop in my left knee. I do not remember a lot of pain, but when I got up, I had no lateral stability in my knee. It was loose and wobbly. I looked down the hill and knew I would never make it to the bottom. Some other skiers stopped to see if I was okay. I was not. I could stand up, but I could not put much weight on my left leg, so they called the ski patrol.

When the ski patrol arrived, they decided to take me down in the sled. Some call it the "ride of shame," but it would have been foolish for me to try to finish the run on a bad knee, especially with my limited skills. At the small Ski Patrol triage room, they determined that I had probably torn my Medial Collateral Ligament, or MCL. But after a short stay in the triage room, and a dose of Tylenol, I was able to walk very gingerly, slowly, and deliberately. So, I was released, deciding not to be transported to the local hospital. I had no idea how much that might cost, and I did not want to find out. Besides, I had come up here by myself, and I did not want to leave my Blazer in the parking lot. Since the injury was to my left knee, I was able to drive home.

After returning my rental skis, a quick trip to a local urgent care center confirmed what they told me on the mountain; I had torn my MCL. After another MRI, I scheduled a visit with Dr. Fuller. He told me that I had a 95 percent tear of the MCL and a torn meniscus. He also told me my MCL tear did not require surgery. I was surprised. How could an injury like this heal itself without surgery? But it did, and in eight weeks, it was completely healed. Now I always wear braces on both knees when I go skiing, just to be cautious.

After that fall in April, my first season was finished and in the books. Even after getting off to such a terrible start, and ending with a serious knee injury, I was generally pleased with my first year. I had a long, long way to go, but I was definitely hooked. I could have easily quit back in December, after that first miserable day, and no one would have thought any less of me. No doubt I would have been applauded for trying at my age. But I did not quit. And by the end of the season, I was already looking forward to the start of the next season.

I have often thought about that first morning on the bunny hill. When I go skiing today, I rarely go past the bunny hills at the different resorts, so I do not know if other seniors ever start skiing on them for their first time. But now I think seeing an old man on the bunny hill would be strange and out of place. I think if I had it to do over again, I probably would have taken Beth's advice and just started on a gentle green hill somewhere. I probably would have fallen just as many times, but I also might have learned to ski a little bit sooner. I am certain that nobody will ever remember that I was that weird old man on the kid's bunny hill that day. I have been back to Copper Mountain many times since that first day, and no one has ever come up to me and said, "Oh, you're that old man from the bunny hill." Thank goodness!

The 2013–2014 ski season was over, but I had lots of work to do between April and November.

MY HOMEMADE SKI MACHINE

With my first ski season now behind me, I got to thinking about what I needed to work on. I never learned to ski in the wedge, or pizza stance like they teach the beginners. From the beginning, I learned to ski using the more advanced parallel stance. So, I wondered if there was a machine that I could train on to practice parallel skiing. I am sure the ski teams used something, but such a machine must be awfully expensive. As it turned out, there are a few machines that do exactly that; they are used by the US and Olympic ski teams, as well as in training facilities across the country. But the model I looked at, made in Europe, cost about twenty-five hundred dollars, after shipping. Basically, these machines use a roller platform that runs side to side on an arched base, attached with bungee cords or something similar, to provide a smooth side-to-side skiing action.

After carefully studying the sleek design of these expensive machines, I wondered if… no way… well, maybe. Maybe I could make my own ski machine. I do not have any pipe bending or welding skills or equipment. But could I fabricate a ski machine out of two-by-fours and plywood to help me practice my parallel skiing technique? I began to turn some ideas over in my mind. First, it would have to be rock solid to support my large frame. Next, it would need to have a smooth action to emulate the parallel skiing motion. The more I thought about it, the more I was convinced I could make such a machine.

I started with the footrests. They each had to be free-swinging, mounted in a frame to allow my feet and knees to rotate as I shifted my weight from side to side.

Next, I built the platform from which the footrests would be suspended. My platform uses the same wheels that the kids use in their little scooters. These wheels are slightly larger than rollerblade wheels and just as durable. They look just like what the commercial machines use and were perfect for my homemade ski machine.

Finally, the base I made is about six feet long with a ten-inch arc. I was not good at geometry in school, so I Googled the geometric formula to mark a ten-inch arc

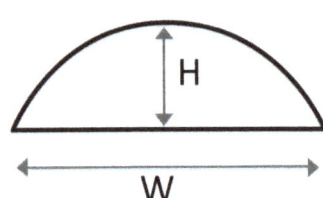

$$R = \frac{H}{2} + \frac{W^2}{8H}$$

W = chord length, H = arc height

on a sheet of ¾-inch plywood. I cut 45-degree angles along the arc line and glued two pieces together, facing each other to form a wedge in which the platform wheels would ride. I made two of these base pieces and tied them together with two-by-fours and heavy 5/8-inch threaded stock.

I then devised a way to attach the bungee cords from the base to the rolling platform.

My machine may not be as sleek and sexy as the commercial model, but it is rock solid, operates very smoothly, and allows me to practice good parallel skiing perfectly. My cost: about a hundred dollars.

My homemade ski machine

However, I soon discovered that my machine had one serious flaw. I did not design a locking mechanism to prevent the platform from moving while getting on and off the machine.

On July 1, 2014, I was using the machine in my basement, as I had done many times before. But this time, when I went to get off, the platform suddenly lurched to the left, throwing me to the right. I lost my balance and fell about two feet, landing on my back on the hard, concrete floor. After about twenty minutes of excruciating pain, I was able to crawl to the bottom of the stairs and get to a semi-upright position, almost. Struggling up each step sent stabbing pain through my back and side. I was finally able to get upstairs to my office chair, which, if I did not move, offered some relief. I debated with myself for about a half-hour whether to go to the hospital or not. Was I having any problem breathing? Was I coughing up any blood? Any other abdominal pain? No, just the pain in my rib cage. So, I decided to drive myself to the Littleton Hospital ER. Remember, Jan has MS and cannot drive, and I did not want to find out how much an ambulance ride would set me back. It is a guy thing. It is a good thing I knew where the hospital was, because everyone knows guys never stop to ask directions. That is also a guy thing.

It was quite painful to walk and get into and out of the Blazer, but once I was sitting, and not moving very much, driving to the hospital was relatively painless and endurable. I got to the hospital without much additional pain. Getting out of the Blazer and walking into the ER was a different story.

A few hours and a couple x-rays later, I was admitted to the hospital with four broken ribs on my right side. As long as I stayed still, the pain was not too bad. My broken ribs were not disjoined, and there was no additional damage such as a punctured or lacerated lung. But it was still a serious and painful injury.

On that first day, any movement was still extremely painful. If I had to cough or sneeze, which, thankfully, I did not do very often, I placed a pillow on my ribcage and held it very tightly and tried to cough very quietly. Transferring for x-rays and a CAT scan onto the cold, hard table on that first night meant using the muscles around my ribcage, which was unbearable.

The next day they placed an epidural anesthesia drip line in my back. This gave me some welcome relief from the tremendous pain, so I could move about in relative comfort. That was, until they removed the line on my last day at the hospital. Then I was rudely reminded that my ribs were not at all healed yet.

The oxycodone and oxycontin pain medication they gave me really upset my stomach and made everything I ate taste like metal. I knew I was hungry, but I had no appetite. I am sure it was the medication, mostly, but I think the hospital food probably had something to do with it as well. Eventually, I could not keep any food down at all. I discovered that vomiting was also very painful.

I spent five days in the hospital and watched the July 4th fireworks displays across Denver from the large visitor lounge windows on my fourth floor.

After I was released, and after spending six more weeks on the mend, I was almost as good as new and looked forward to the beginning of the next ski season.

Even after my accident, I still used the machine; it helped to retain the muscle memory in the off-season. It is a very solid machine, and I have since added a locking mechanism, so the platform does not move when getting on or off.

CHRISTY SPORTS POWDER DAZE

By Labor Day, I was more than ready to get back to skiing. But the first real ski day was still about three months away. Christy Sports, by far my favorite ski store, has an annual Labor Day sales event called Powder Daze. In this event, they sell last year's equipment at bargain prices to make room for this year's new stuff.

I was now committed to doing the skiing thing, and I was tired of renting skis and returning them at the end of each day. So, I purchased a pair of Atomic skis and Solomon ski bindings. I also bought a new pair of Spyder ski pants because my cheap Walmart pants had split open when I fell at Loveland. I had already bought a Giro helmet, goggles, Goode carbon fiber poles, and Nordic boots earlier this year. I was now fully equipped to continue with this commitment. No more rentals!

I also invested in a GoPro Hero3+ action camera. I take this camera every time I go skiing, mounted on my helmet. I have captured many runs, as well as my falls. Sometimes it is easy to forget to turn the camera off at the end of the run, so I've captured quite a few trips up the ski lift as well. Though not as exciting, these accidental chair lift videos capture some beautiful and peaceful moments from the day on the mountain.

Now I was ready to start my second season of skiing.

I think the most important thing in skiing is you have to be having fun. If you're having fun, then everything else will come easy to you.
—Lindsey Vonn

SECOND YEAR (2014–2015)

My second year had so much promise. My confidence and optimism were through the roof. I had my season pass for Copper Mountain and Winter Park, plus a 4-PAK for Loveland. I could not wait to hit the slopes again. I was healed from my spring and summer injuries, and I was ready to get back on the mountain.

In November, Beth was home on leave, and we went to Copper Mountain again. I had my day all planned out. I had been working out for much of the summer and had studied hundreds of instructional videos. I was going to tear up the slopes this year. I guess I forgot that I still did not know how to stop.

This first day of the new season was bright and sunny. The air was crisp and cold, and the snow was groomed and crisp beneath my skis, a picture-perfect ski day in the Rockies. After getting off the American Flyer lift, we started down the Coppertone run. This is a gentle green run and great for practicing techniques. It is long, wide, well groomed, and not so steep that your speed quickly gets away from you. Yet it is still steep enough to practice your skills.

Starting down this run, however, I soon realized that my optimism far exceeded my limited abilities. Almost immediately, my ski tips were flopping all over the place, and stopping still meant long gentle turns until I was eventually skiing uphill, unless I ran out of real estate. The other option was to just go faster and faster down the hill until I fell again.

To make things worse, we somehow got over to the American Eagle side of the mountain, which is generally steeper with mostly blue and black runs. By now, I had already fallen several times. No injuries, but painful, nonetheless. Not being able to stop was now a real problem. My confidence was gone, and I was sore and frustrated beyond imagination. And to make things worse, the very last part of the run was still ahead.

I had fallen once again at the top of the hill that overlooked the American Eagle lift. I was now sitting on the crest, gazing down on skiers waiting in line to get back on the lift. My skis were laying lifeless on the snow in front of me, and Beth had come over to provide encouragement and some final instructions on the best way to get down to the bottom. This last section was short, but steep and fast, and I was afraid that I would just rumble into the crowd, still unable to stop on demand.

I had a few options. I could just sit here until the season was over and simply walk to the bottom of the hill on dry ground when no one was watching. This did not seem very practical, and I quickly dismissed the idea. Another option was to call the ski patrol and get another ride on the sled for the final three hundred feet to the bottom.

Okay, I never actually entertained these ideas. I just had to get back into my skis and shoot down the hill, hoping for the best.

I made it down the hill without running into anyone, but my day was over after just one long miserable run. I was now seriously thinking about selling all my new equipment and just calling it quits. Maybe skiing was not for me after all. All my optimism and enthusiasm had been crushed on the first run of the season. I was so stiff and sore from falling down the mountain over and over again, that I asked Beth to drive home. It was a really bad day.

But Beth has always been a source of encouragement and motivation since my earliest days of skiing. On the long drive home, she did not dwell on today's bad run but rather talked about the progress I had made to this point.

She reminded me of the earliest days when I could barely stand on my skis. She reminded me that nobody ever starts skiing at my age, and that there would always be bad days. She recalled the run we did in my first year going down an easy green switchback trail where I had fallen many times but got up each time and kept going. She then reminded me that at the end of my first season, I was going down long green runs under control without falling. Sure, I had much more to learn, but it would take time, practice, and a lot of patience. It does not all come together right away. With each season you always make improvements and get better. So, on this first day of just my second season,

I should not discount the progress I have made so far. Besides, first days of the season are never the best. It always takes a few ski days to get back to good form after the long summer. One bad day did not mean I should give up. Things would get better. She was right.

Winter Park: Learning to Stop

On December 16, we went to Winter Park. This time, we worked on one thing only—stopping. We went up the Zephyr Express lift and came down March Hare, a green run, but narrow, fast, and fun. Starting at the top, Beth had me go down the hill about a hundred feet or so and turn to stop. I turned, but did not stop, at first. We did this exercise over and over. She patiently stuck with me all the way down the hill, and after a few more runs doing this drill, I started to get the hang of the hockey stop. Once it clicked, I was excited to try it again and again for the rest of the day. I still had a lot of work to do, but this was a huge game-changer for me.

When you can stop on demand, the mountain opens up. You are no longer intimidated because you have no control. You begin to pick up your speed because you know you can hit the brakes if you have to. It may sound a little bit counter-intuitive, but after an afternoon of stopping, I felt my confidence coming back in a flood.

I got to drive home this time. This was good day.

Winter Park: Cranmer and the ER

Cranmer is a long blue run that I enjoy going down at least a few times whenever I go to Winter Park. But that was not always the case. After learning to stop on demand, Beth and I returned to Winter Park on December 26. Up to this point, I had not gone down any blue runs, except on that first day at Copper, by mistake. As part of my improvement plan, Beth wanted me to compare a blue run to the green runs that I was now comfortable with. That sounded like a good idea, and I was up to the challenge.

Cranmer is very wide and long, and a good run for practicing intermediate skills. It is groomed and easy to navigate, even for entry-level intermediate skiers. And wide often means not as crowded.

So, after a few warm-up runs down the now-familiar March Hare, we eased onto the turnoff to go down Cranmer. I must say that the view from the top of Cranmer is spectacular. It never gets old.

But I was still nervous, since this was my first time going down this blue run, or any blue run, intentionally. I knew I had to start doing more blue runs and that if I took this one easy (after all, I was now a master of the hockey stop), I would have no problem. As I started down the hill, I began to pick up speed and could feel the wind in my face. It was exhilarating. As I picked up speed, I could feel my turns finally working at my command. Easing over each new crescent, I no longer felt the fear and trepidation that I often felt before as a beginner. I could see the entire hill spread out before me, inviting me to go faster and faster. I was now trusting my skis and my skills. It was spectacular.

For the first time, I really began to feel quite comfortable and in control. I began to understand the thrill that experienced skiers feel on each run. This looked like it was going to be a great run.

There is a term skiers use when the snow seems to jump up and grab one of your skis, violently pulling it to the side. They say, "My ski caught an edge." Sometimes you can recover, and sometimes you just go down. It usually happens when you are running flat on your skis. It seldom happens when you are turning and using the edge of your skis. It has happened to all skiers and snowboarders, and everyone knows the term because everyone has experienced it at one time or another. At slower speeds, it is just embarrassing. At higher speeds, it is frightening and dangerous. And when I have one of those senior moments when I am just walking down a sidewalk or across a parking lot and suddenly trip or fall, I just say, "My shoe caught an edge." Everyone understands the term.

As I was going down Cranmer, picking up more speed, and feeling really good about this run, that's exactly what happened to me; my ski caught an edge. In an instant, my right ski was violently pulled to the right, and I went down hard, with my right shoulder taking the full force of the fall. It all happened in a split-second. I heard a loud pop, followed by excruciating pain, much more pain than when I tore my MCL at Loveland back in April.

I do not know how far I tumbled, but when I stopped, I was sitting up looking down the hill, staring at my ski boots with no skis. The pain was intense! I started to hyper-ventilate, and I thought for sure I had just broken my collarbone. As I carefully tried to move my arm and shoulder around, I could feel something loose and grinding inside, and it was not a good feeling. Just what I needed, another serious ski injury.

Apparently, it was a spectacular fall because a small crowd was soon gathered around me. One person brought my skis down from up the hill. Someone else asked if I was okay.

"Did you hurt your head?"

No, I hurt my shoulder.

"Do you need us to call ski patrol?"

Not yet.

After several minutes, I was able to stand up. The intense pain had subsided some, and I could move my shoulder a little bit, although it still felt like something was loose and definitely out of place. I knew I was not going to be doing push-ups anytime soon. Remembering my ride of shame at Loveland earlier this year, I decided to try skiing on down to the bottom of the hill. I carefully locked back into my skis and started down the hill, slowly, carefully, and stopping often. I met Beth partway down the hill and told her what happened. I was eventually able to ski on down to the bottom of the hill, which was maybe about a mile. But at least my turns were still working, I could stop on command, and I felt like I was still in control. By the time we got to the bottom of the hill, the pain had returned, this time as a dull throb.

At first, I thought we could just go home, where I could put some ice on my shoulder and go to the doctor the next day. But about halfway through the village on the way back to the parking lot, the increasing pain gave me second thoughts. So, we turned around and walked back to the Denver Health ER station at the other end of the village.

The Denver Health Winter Park Medical Center is a well-equipped, Level 1 trauma center. When we entered the ER, they asked me what happened and then proceeded with their usual triage, filling out forms, taking my pulse, and checking my temperature. When they saw my shoulder, with the end of my collarbone sticking up under the skin, they put an ice pack on it to stop the swelling.

Then they asked the most important medical emergency question of all, "Do you have insurance?"

After giving them my insurance card and filling out some more paperwork, I was whisked away to radiology for an x-ray. The x-ray showed that I had suffered a Type III shoulder separation. This was the same shoulder that had been surgically repaired two years earlier, although a torn rotator cuff is not the same as a shoulder separation. A shoulder separation tears the ligaments that attach the collarbone to the shoulder blade. That was why the end of my collarbone was now jutting up a couple of inches under my skin.

There was nothing more that the ER could do for me, so they put my arm in a sling and sent me on my way. Obviously, Beth drove home that evening, and I had to explain to Jan how I managed to suffer yet another serious injury early in my ski career.

Back at the office, Pam, a co-worker and good friend, tried unsuccessfully to hide her laughter as I explained why I now resembled the hunchback of Notre Dame. As long as I was generally ok, she always thought it was funny whenever I came to work after getting hurt while skiing over the weekend. Torn MCL, broken ribs, shoulder separation, all elicited a good laugh at my expense. But the worst was yet to come.

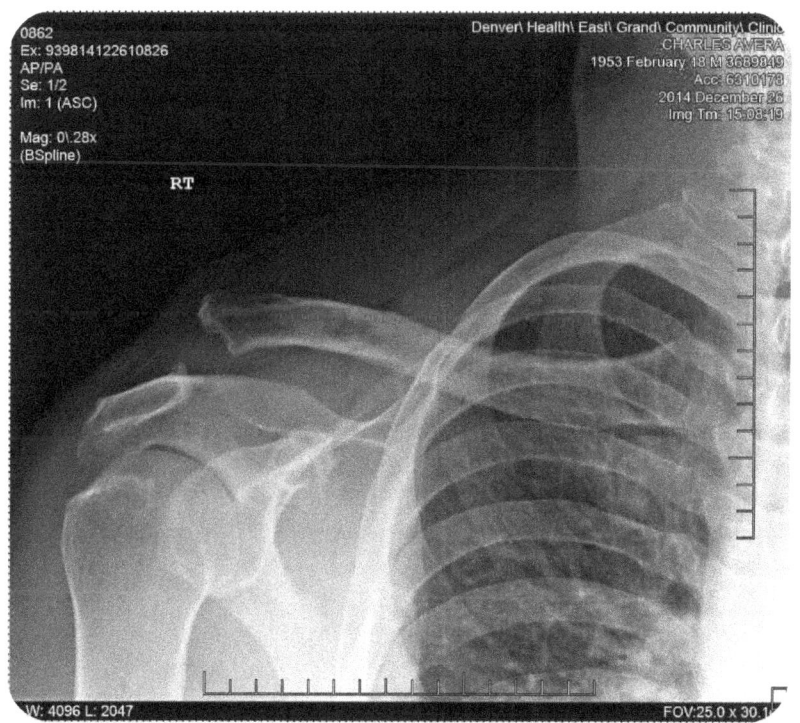

It was two weeks before I was finally able to see Dr. Fuller, again. He told me that this injury would be permanent. The pain would go away, mostly, but the collarbone would be permanently separated from the shoulder blade, and that big lump on my shoulder would give me bragging rights and bursitis for the rest of my life. He was right. I still have a big lump at the end of my collar bone. But a few weeks later, I was able to get back on the slopes again. This would not be the last time I fell while skiing, but it would be the last injury I would sustain for the next two years.

I have skied down Cranmer many times since then and thoroughly enjoy the thrill of this run every time. However, each time I go down it, I remember the day that my ski caught an edge and I went down hard. Apart from my pride, it was the most severe injury I had suffered while skiing. Now I feel like I own that hill, and I can fearlessly do that run anytime. But on December 26, 2014, the hill owned me.

In January and February, I enjoyed three uneventful, injury-free days at Winter Park, Loveland, and Copper Mountain. I was able to practice my skills and work on some flaws on their long, gentle runs. At this point, uneventful was good, and more ski days only helped. I was now getting comfortable going down the runs, able to control my speed and stop when I wanted to. I had come a long way since that first miserable run of the season at Copper Mountain.

Breckenridge: March 2015

A bad day skiing still beats a good day at the office.

In March, some friends from work and I took the day off and went to Breckenridge. Floyd and Fernando were both beginner-level skiers and were not quite up to taking on the more aggressive runs today. Lisa, on the other hand, started skiing at a young age and found the easy green runs quite tame and not very challenging or fun at all.

After the first run down an easy green hill, Floyd and Fernando decided to pack it in and enjoy the rest of the day back at the lodge. So, Lisa and I spent the rest of the day exploring some of the other more aggressive trails that Breckenridge had to offer.

I have often said that even a bad day of skiing is better than a good day at work. And this was truly a good day of skiing. I had never been to Breckenridge before, but I had heard about the long and wide runs there and was not disappointed at all.

After one of our early runs, Lisa and I got separated. That is when I discovered a fun blue run called Northstar. It was wide and long and from the top looked very steep. I stood at the top for several minutes, trying to muster the courage to plunge over the edge. But when I did finally start down the hill, it was incredibly exciting and fun.

It was about a mile back down to the lifts and challenging all the way. But I took the hill in good form and was thrilled all the way down. At the bottom I connected up with Lisa again, and convinced her to go back up to Northstar with me. At the top, I hesitated once again. Yes, I was still scared. But from the corner of my eye, I saw Lisa come up to the edge and shoot on down the hill. So much for my fear and hesitation! I pushed over the edge and shot down the hill, trying to catch up with her. This was another great run down the long, steep slope.

We did mostly blue runs, but I also did my first black diamond run. We did the Spruce run three times that day. As far as black diamonds go, Spruce had a reputation; it was the easiest black diamond at Breckenridge. But it was still a black diamond; long, steep, and fast. And at my experience level, it was all I could handle.

Lisa was able to see how I was skiing throughout the day. When the day was over, I asked her if she had any tips for me. She told me, "Charlie, your form and technique are okay. You just need to put more miles on the mountain."

That was some good advice from a friend. In the seasons since that trip to Breckenridge, the miles on the mountain have been the biggest factor that elevated my skills and confidence.

By April, my second ski season had come to an end. I went to Loveland one last time with Becky. However, by this late date, the snow was soft and mushy, and skiing that day was just not much fun at all.

But after that terrible first day at Copper Mountain, wondering if I would even continue skiing at all, the season turned out to be a good one. I still needed many more miles, but I was now comfortable on the slopes and already looking forward to the start of the next season. Summer, ugh.

Remember, if you don't do it this year, you'll be one year older when you do
—Warren Miller

THIRD YEAR (2015–2016)

For those of us who love the snow and skiing, April to November is a long seven months. And I really do not like hot weather at all. I passed the dog days of summer working, caregiving, mowing the lawn, pulling weeds, working out, fixing things around the house, and going on a few hikes. Really, I was just staying busy doing anything to pass the time. July dragged into August, and August melted into September. Finally, the Christy Sports Powder Daze sale came around again on Labor Day. It was still sizzling outside, but the calendar said that summer was almost over, and the new ski season was now just a few short months away.

All I really needed at Powder Daze this year was to get my Super Pass for Copper Mountain and Winter Park. I also wanted to buy another 4-PAK for Loveland. Otherwise, I did not need any more equipment, and I could have left Christy Sports with just the ski passes. But to get out of the store, I had to walk past the racks with all the nice, brightly colored ski jackets. I can usually pass this section, because as a large person, I know that there will probably not be a jacket that will fit me. I know because I had already looked many times before.

But this time, there was one jacket that seemed to jump off the rack and beg me to take it home. It was my size and the color I wanted, and it had all the features of a top-quality ski jacket: lots of zippered pockets, snow skirt, fleece lined hood, and zippered vents for warmer days. And when I tried it on, it was a perfect fit. Skiers never really need a good reason to buy new equipment. Father's Day, birthdays, Christmas, Tuesday, Saturday… any occasion will do. So, I brought that bright orange Spyder jacket home with me, and from the first day of my third season, I was skiing in style. No doubt it made me a much better skier.

I would definitely consider my third season a breakout year. It was not perfect, and there were still some frustrations, but by the end of this season, I was skiing any blue runs as well as some more black diamonds with confidence. And I have the video to prove it.

This season finally started when Beth and I went to Loveland along with a friend of hers. The only run that was open this early in the season was a steep slope off Lift 1 called Spillway. A few years later, Lift 1 would be replaced with a new lift called Chet's Dream.

View of Spillway approaching the top of Chet's Dream lift. It is a steep hill. Joe Alonzo, January 18, 2019, *Ski Loveland Chet's Dream*, viewed February 10, 2019, <https://www.youtube.com/watch?v=MKuHk6DKh5s>. Image used with permission.

Spillway is a short run, and I suppose that is the only reason it is classified as a blue run instead of a black diamond. Standing at the top, gazing down the steep incline can be very scary for new skiers. I have watched skiers and snowboarders hesitate at the edge for several minutes before taking the plunge. I have also watched many just go on down the service road and take the easier switchback to get to the lower runs. And that group included me. This hill is steep and extremely fast, and a gateway to the other runs that feed into Home Run, the final trail that takes you back to the chairlift at the base of the mountain. But today, there was no other way down. It was early in the season and the other trails had not opened yet.

I had watched many videos of skiers going down this hill, but I had always avoided it because it was just too intimidating for me. And for the first run of my third season, it was still very formidable. I parked at the top for several minutes, mustering up the courage to ease over the edge. Once I started down the hill, there was no turning back.

We went down Spillway four times that day, but I only made it down once without falling. Because it was steep for me, my skis just slid out from under me while I was trying to slow down. In my fourth year, I would learn why this was happening and how to correct it. But compared to tumbling and sliding down the side of the hill out of control, hoping you can get up again when you finally stop, I do not really think of that as falling any more. So, on the first three runs, I just did not make it down without ending up on my rear.

It was still a great day of skiing, and the 2015–2016 season had now begun. The long, hot summer was finally over.

Skiing with Ravi

This year, I also started skiing with a colleague from work. For his day job, Ravi Shankar was a software tester, and I got to know him when we worked together on some projects. I also discovered that he was a novice skier. Ravi is quite an interesting person. He is originally from India but spent many years in New Zealand and Australia. And he is about thirty years younger than me. When I first met him, I asked him if he had ever heard of another Ravi Shankar, the famous Indian sitar player who was quite popular in the mid-sixties.

Without hesitation, he said, "Yes, that was my grandfather." Then a big grin came across his face as he burst into jolly laughter. Obviously, this was not the first time he had been asked if they were related.

This was Ravi's second year skiing, and he wanted to advance his skills. Several of my friends either moved away or decided to skip this season, and Beth was not able to take leave very often. So, Ravi and I spent many great days skiing at Winter Park and Copper Mountain. I found myself helping him improve his skills, and in the process, I improved mine as well. He had several areas to work on, and I often skied behind him, capturing his runs with my GoPro action camera. Honestly, I found it a little bit difficult to ski slowly behind him, as he was still somewhat timid about going faster down the hill. In fact, this was one of the things that was hindering his improvement. I often skied on ahead of him and then videoed him as he came down the hill. But we both had a great time, and we both improved significantly this year.

Imagine, this old grandpa from the bunny hill now coaching my friend through his own skiing experience. I think I have certainly come a long way indeed.

Focused Improvement

When I first started skiing, my only goal was to get down the mountain safely, without falling or hurting myself. Since I did not get my GoPro until after my first season, I did not have anything but my memories to know what mistakes I was making. Of course, taking videos with a camera mounted on my helmet did not provide as much insight as someone taking videos while skiing beside or behind me. And since Beth was not into doing action videos, I had very few videos to study. But with the GoPro's wide-angle lens, I was often able to capture what my ski tips and hands were doing, and my shadow also provided some insight on bright days, as long as the sun was behind me. These were all helpful when analyzing what areas to improve. They also provided some great shots when I fell.

But the videos did show some progress over the past two seasons. Early on, it was obvious that I had little control. My turns were jerky, I had problems stopping, and my ski tips were flopping all over the place. Skiing like that made it hard to focus on any one area to improve. All my flaws converged on each run, and I just had too much information to process simultaneously to work on specific areas for improvement. The goal at that time was to get to the bottom of the hill without falling. But as I became more comfortable skiing down a hill, I could better isolate and assess specific areas that still needed more work. This year gave me that opportunity. I was comfortable going down the hills, and I could now begin to isolate different things that I still needed to work on. And I had a lot of fun at the same time.

Left Turn Stopping

As I learned to stop at the beginning of my second season, I found that I was always turning to my right to make the stop. I got to where I could stop nearly on a dime. It was fun hitting the brakes and sending snow flying. This skill gave me the confidence to take on most runs and truly opened the whole mountain to me. But trying to stop by turning to my left was a different story altogether. I was very right-turn dominant. I do not know if that is a real term, or if it is just my own made-up skiing technobabble, but it simply means I still could not stop very well by turning to my left. Instead of stopping, I just kept turning until I was eventually going back uphill, just like in the early days. If I tried to stop hard, I would lose my balance and sometimes fall or start sliding down the hill backward. If I tried to stop beside my friends, I would sometimes run into them or just ski right past them. It was so embarrassing.

So, this year, I set out to work on that. I made a conscious effort to stop by turning to my left instead of my right every time I could. It is not exactly like writing left-handed if you are naturally right-handed. But there is a tendency to be naturally one-side dominant for stopping and switching to the other side is far less natural. I worked on this all season, often stopping when I did not have to, even on steep slopes, just to practice. A lot of it was just a matter of getting used to this new motion and fine-tuning my balance. Repetition was the key. And with a lot of repetition and practice, stopping to my left now almost feels as natural as stopping to my right.

Smooth Turns and Speed Control

My turns were still not smooth. To control your speed, you constantly turn from side to side as you go down the hill. You want to make smooth, connected S-shaped turns, gliding smoothly down the mountain. I constantly worked on this throughout the season. Early on, I would start a run by pointing my skis diagonally across the hill in one direction and picking up some speed. Then I would hit the brakes during a quick, sharp Z turn, and go back across the hill in the other direction. This is how I would control my speed while working my way down the hill.

This was poor technique. I wanted to control my speed by making smooth, linked S turns, instead of the sharp, jerky Z turns that I was doing. I noticed that what I thought I was doing and what I was really doing were often two different things. While I thought I was making wide, smooth S turns, the videos showed clearly that I was still making short, quick, and jerky Z turns. But with practice and repetition came confidence, so that by the end of this third year, I was beginning to make better, smoother, linked turns, controlling my speed, and enjoying each run more and more. But this new motion did not come easily, and at the end of the season, I still had more work to do on my turns.

Increasing My Speed

To me, screaming down the mountain is not as important as skiing with good form and technique. I will leave the speed to the kids. I ski to enjoy it. And I certainly do enjoy it. Okay, I admit it, I am still scared to go really fast. I do not think I can take too many more injuries. That is why I hit the brakes and made jerky Z turns. But good speed is important to make good turns down the mountain. You just cannot turn going slow.

This year, I discovered that as my experience, confidence, and comfort increased, so did my speed. As my turns became smoother, my speed naturally increased, and my fear greatly subsided.

Nobody said it would be easy. They only said it would be worth it.
—Anonymous

FOURTH YEAR (2016–2017)

The 2016–2017 season got off to a late start. November came and went with temps in the 70s and 80s in Denver. Opening day at all the resorts kept getting delayed, again and again. I knew winter and opening day would eventually arrive, but skiers and snowboarders everywhere were growing frustrated and impatient. But what can you do? Opening day would get here when it wanted to.

My opening day for this season came on January 10 at Winter Park, much later than past years. Our Indian summer was finally over, and temps on this day were hovering around 12 degrees. When I am skiing down the hill, I am somewhat oblivious to the low temperatures. But on days like this one, it is hard to enjoy a full day on the slopes. Today, the ride to the top of the lift in the open chair was brutally cold. But the first day of a new season is always an exciting time, and today was no exception.

I had one goal for this year: conquering my fears. There were certain runs at my favorite resorts that were still intimidating to me. White Rabbit and Jabberwocky at Winter Park, Bittersweet and Main Vein at Copper, and Mary Jane and Parsenn Bowl on the Mary Jane side of Winter Park, to mention a few.

The first few ski days this season were not any different from the end of last season. Steep hills and bumpy terrain still intimidated me. I seemed to have reached a plateau. So, I decided to take another lesson. Winter Park had a special program for older skiers called Platinum Tracks. The class met early on Wednesdays, taking advantage of the freshly groomed and relatively empty trails. I watched some online videos of this class and saw a bunch of guys learning new techniques and refining their skills under the expert tutelage of an experienced instructor. Maybe this is what I needed. So, I signed up for a class on January 18.

Getting up to Winter Park in time for the 8:45 start meant getting on the road by six in the morning. That is earlier than I leave for work most days. As I expected, traffic up I-70 this early on a weekday was not a problem, as it sometimes is, and I arrived early enough to get my class pass and grab a light breakfast.

At 8:45, we gathered between the Zephyr and Arrow lifts across from the Balcony House cafeteria. It was a moderately large group, but the instructors were flexible.

"How many of you want to learn how to ski moguls and bumps, and how many want to improve your technique?"

We were separated into these two groups. I wanted to see if I could learn something new to improve and refine my technique, so I went with that group. Maybe I could learn to do moguls some other time, but today, I just wanted to improve my technique.

It is usually hard to guess a person's age when they are bundled for skiing and hiding behind goggles and a helmet. But I soon learned that I was grouped together with six other older ladies, part of a close-knit senior skiing and community service group. Okay, let me just see how this goes.

Talking with a few of them on the long rides up the mountain, I learned that several of them had been skiing since the 1960s. I thought they would be advanced, seasoned skiers, looking to step up their game even more. I imagined they would be tearing down the mountain at a pace even the young skiers and snowboarders would find hard to keep up with. Not quite. It turned out that they were just kind, senior ladies who only wanted to ski slowly down gentle slopes, making good turns along the way. I soon felt like I was skiing with Betty White and five of her friends.

But they all had a good time talking about how nice things were back in the sixties and how scared they were of how fast the kids ski and snowboard today. Bob, the instructor, kept telling us how he had been at Winter Park for forty years, except for a few years when he helped set up another resort; he even had a ski run named after him. It was certainly an over-fifty group. But we all had fun skiing slowly down some gentle blue runs. Oh, and Bob also taught us a few things about skiing too.

He told all of us what we were doing wrong. We all wondered how he could possibly know what we were doing wrong, since he was always skiing in front of us. But he knew exactly what we were doing. Maybe he just knew because he had been an instructor for so long and knew what mistakes all skiers make in his classes. But regardless of how he knew, he hit the nail on the head. All of us were leaning back on our skis. This was all I got out of the class, but it was all I needed.

Bob drilled into us to lean slightly forward on our skis when going down a hill by always keeping our hands out in front of us. It is often the subtle things that we overlook that make a big difference. The idea is to always remain perpendicular to your skis, keeping balanced over their centers, even as the slope increases. This is not natural. In fact, it is a terrifying concept to new skiers.

New skiers think, *"I'm plunging down this hill, terrified and out of control, and now you want me to do what? Lean forward and go even faster?"* All new skiers lean back in their skis as the hill becomes steeper. It is a natural reaction to fear. But leaning forward is critical to keeping balanced over your skis and actually gives you much more control as you go down the mountain. Leaning back on your skis nearly always guarantees losing control and increases your chances of falling.

Bob showed us how to control our speed by making smooth turns down the mountain instead of leaning back on our skis.

After a few runs, it all clicked. With this small change, I was finally skiing gracefully down the mountain, leaning forward correctly on my skis, hands out in front, controlling my speed, and having more fun than I had ever had before. Suddenly, I was hitting the hills with confidence, without hesitating at the top. Now I really had a difficult time staying back with the other ladies. I did not take this lesson to learn how to ski slowly. I had learned what I came for, and by the end of the class, I was ready and eager to take on even bigger challenges.

White Rabbit, Jabberwocky, Cheshire Cat, Mary Jane, and Parsenn Bowl

On February 16, Beth and I spent the day at Winter Park again. It was another picture-perfect day and turned out to be probably my best skiing day so far.

White Rabbit

We started the day going down White Rabbit, a great blue run next to March Hare and Cranmer. Early in the day, this run was well groomed and nearly pristine. Visibility was simply forever and going down the hill was like gliding across a smooth lake in the early morning. The techniques I learned from the Platinum Tracks class worked perfectly, and I felt in total control, like I had never felt before. The only problem was that the run was over way too soon. This was a great warm-up run and perfectly set the rhythm and mood for the rest of the day.

Gliding down White Rabbit

Jabberwocky

After White Rabbit, we went down Jabberwocky, the next hill over, slightly steeper, and more aggressive. This run was just as fun as White Rabbit, and like White Rabbit, it was also over way too soon. My confidence was building quickly.

Gentle run-out after White Rabbit and Jabberwocky from the Olympia Express lift

Cheshire Cat

Of the five hills off the Zephyr and Olympia Express lifts, Cheshire Cat is perhaps the most challenging and aggressive. It is classified as a blue/black run and still a challenge for intermediate skiers. After building my confidence on White Rabbit and Jabberwocky, I was up to the challenge of doing Cheshire Cat. Since I had never been down this run, I still hesitated at the top and approached it cautiously. But at the bottom, I thought, *"What's the big deal? That was like any other blue run I've done."* It was really fun, and I wanted to do it again, but Beth and I had more adventures to do today.

But Cheshire Cat also has a reputation, as I would discover a month later. Today, however, this run became one more box checked on my skiing bucket list.

Midway down Cheshire Cat

Mary Jane

After Cheshire Cat, we took the Olympia Express lift to the lower part of the Whistle Stop run, a green run that borders the Winter Park and Mary Jane regions. The Mary Jane region at Winter Park is known for its more aggressive and often ungroomed runs. The Mary Jane run is just one of many blue and black runs in the Mary Jane region; it is very popular with intermediate skiers.

Perry's Peak (Bear Claw Mountain) from the top of Olympia
Express lift before going down Mary Jane

Beth and I had done Mary Jane a couple years before. Since I was still a beginner back then, the run was really challenging, and I took a nasty spill after hitting a small ravine. I did not hurt myself, but the memory of that fall lingered for a long time. Today, I had much more confidence and control, so we eased onto Mary Jane from Whistle Stop and enjoyed another fantastic run. Next, we took the Super Gauge Express lift back to the top for one more run before stopping for lunch. Super Gauge took us even higher up the mountain than the Olympia lift, so we were able to drop into Mary Jane on the black diamond part at the top for our second run. It is easy to understand why Mary Jane is such a popular attraction for Colorado skiers.

Starting down Mary Jane

Parsenn Bowl

At an elevation of 12,060 feet, Parsenn Bowl is the crown of the Winter Park Ski Resort. After a quick run down the Roundhouse trail from the Super Gauge lift, it is just a few hundred feet over to the Panorama Express lift. Pano is the only lift to the top of Parsenn Bowl, and it is often closed due to high winds and poor visibility. And when it is open, there is usually a long line before you can get onto your chair, proving that this is one of the most popular destinations at Winter Park for intermediate and advanced skiers.

The gentle and peaceful ride to the top provides the most spectacular views of the entire park.

Approaching top of Parsenn Bowl on Panorama Express lift

High above the tree line, the top of Parsenn Bowl is so beautiful, we did not just jump off the lift and immediately shoot down the hill. We took some time to take in the moment and get some pictures, because words would simply not be adequate to describe this place.

View from top of Parsenn Bowl

The run from the top of Parsenn Bowl is deceptive. The top of the bowl is a vast, open area with no trees to provide any perspective. The hill quickly becomes steeper than it first seems, and your speed can get away from you very quickly. But with the techniques and skills I learned this year, I am beginning to ski steeper slopes with a healthy mix of aggression and caution. Today, we did four runs from the top of Parsenn, and each one was truly exhilarating.

Beth starting down Parsenn Bowl

These four runs, plus the two runs down Mary Jane and seven runs down the other Winter Park blue slopes, made this day the best day of my short skiing career so far. We did thirteen runs for nearly twenty miles. If this day had been my last for this season, I would have been content, and this season would have been a total success. This was just one of those rare days of skiing that make the best memories.

I would never guess that I had only two days of skiing left before my fourth season would come to an abrupt and painful end.

Loveland Ski Area: Paying It Forward

On the drive home from Winter Park, Beth thought it would be great if we could bring Riley, Becky's young, almost teenage daughter, up to the mountain to learn how to ride a snowboard. But Beth

had to return to her base in New Mexico and did not know when she would be able to come back to Colorado. Since time was running out for this season, I decided to take Riley to Loveland for a day of snowboard instruction.

I like the Loveland Valley Ski School. I have taken several lessons there, and Riley's mom also took lessons there. They have excellent programs for teaching beginners of all ages.

Riley had no idea what was up. We had secretly planned for her to spend the night at our house on Friday. Thinking it was just a long-overdue family visit, we totally surprised her when we revealed the plans for the next day. And so early on Saturday, March 4, we made the drive up I-70 to Loveland Valley for her to begin her own winter snow adventure.

The beginning snowboard lesson at Loveland Valley is an all-day class where the kids are pried away from their parents and grandparents early in the morning, spend the day learning to strap into a snowboard, and end it with riding down the short beginner hill. This was the same hill I struggled with four years earlier.

Parents and grandparents are only allowed to watch from a distance. It is an effective technique. The kids quickly learn that for these few hours, the instructor is the master, and the parents and grandparents do not interfere.

By the end of the day, Riley had learned the basics of riding a snowboard and could not contain her excitement. She was off to a great start and could not wait to go up again with her aunt Beth, and maybe Grandpa too.

Loveland Valley: Lift 3

So, what does the Loveland Ski School do with all these parents and grandparents who can only watch the kids from a distance? The school is really smart. They give them Lift 3.

Lift 3 is in the Loveland Ski School area and provides access to several aggressive blue ski runs, including a few steep, off-limits slalom runs used by different ski teams. Lift 3 is the Valley's great secret getaway for the parents.

Approaching the top of Lift 3 at Loveland Valley

Four years earlier, Beth had convinced me to try going down Zig-Zag, a green switchback trail off of Lift 3. For her, Lift 3 was the only access to any blue runs without driving back up to the Basin. She thought we could go down Zig-Zag, where I could practice my beginner's skills. Sometimes these switchback service roads are difficult for beginners because they are narrow with steep drop-offs on the sides and sharp turns where the trail switches back. But she was confident that I could go down without any problem. I was not so sure. "Going down" was the operative phrase here. I was still so new to skiing at that point that I must have fallen a couple dozen times before getting to the bottom. Although this run would be quite easy for me today, on that day it was, well, a challenge to, say the least.

So, for four years, I had always wanted to go back up and conquer this hill on my terms. Today, I had the opportunity to do just that.

Starting down Switchback from Lift 3

I was able to go down Double Dip and Switchback six times while Riley was in her class. Switchback is the name of the long and steep run that goes straight from the top of Lift 3 to the bottom, and not a reference to the service road I struggled with four years earlier. Double Dip is as steep as Spillway at the Basin but is divided by a leg of Zig-Zag about halfway down the run.

Today, I was able to jump onto these runs without any hesitation and smoothly glide down them in good form and, most importantly, without any fear. I did not even bother to go down Zig-Zag where I had struggled so much before.

These six runs more than made up for the single miserable run I did four years earlier. I was gratified because I had worked hard over the past three years to be able to jump onto these steep hills without any fear or hesitation.

It was a great day for both Riley and me.

The Last Day of the Season: March 11

A week later I decided to go to Winter Park by myself. As my skill and experience increased over the seasons, I began skiing by myself more often when I could not find anyone to go with me. And I began to feel quite comfortable doing so.

Saturday, March 11, began like any other ski day for me. I got up early and checked the weather report for Winter Park. The forecast was for warmer temperatures and partly cloudy skies. Spring conditions meant soft snow, but nothing to be overly concerned with. Besides, this would give me an opportunity to practice skiing in these spring conditions, something I really needed to work on.

The now-familiar drive up I-70 was uneventful. A few snow flurries gave way to clearing skies, and it looked like it was going to be another bluebird day at Winter Park.

Taking Exit 232 off I-70, I left the normal heavy traffic behind and started up Highway 40 for the quiet twenty-six-mile drive to Winter Park. After going through Empire, I started through the hairpin turns to Berthoud Pass and the Continental Divide. As the elevation increased, so did the snow left over from a storm that had passed through earlier in the week.

Up ahead, I noticed a big snowplow coming down the hill. As the truck passed me, I heard a loud "CRACK" and glanced over to see a big new star crack in my windshield. Perhaps a sign of things to come? Nah. I do not believe in omens.

From Berthoud Pass, it was only eleven miles to Winter Park and another great day of skiing.

After parking, I took the small cabriolet lift from the parking lot, gently riding above the resort, and ending up at the edge of the village. From there I made my way down through the village to the base of the mountain.

I buckled my boots, locked into my skis, adjusted my electronics, and got in line at the Zephyr Lift. I was ready for another awesome day at Winter Park.

I started the day by going down the now-familiar White Rabbit and Jabberwocky runs. But with the warmer conditions, the snow was soft and grabby. I took these runs slowly and cautiously. My skis were just not turning in sync with each other. I felt like I was skiing in oatmeal. But I made it down these first two runs without any other issues. They were not the fast, crisp runs like I went down just a week ago at Loveland, but it is always fun being on the slopes.

I have heard people talk about how much they really like skiing in these spring conditions. Skiing in these conditions requires a different skill set, and I just needed to get the hang of it. And that only comes with experience. Today was a perfect day to practice and build these new skills. But as I watched other skiers effortlessly plow through the thick, grabby snow, I felt like such a beginner again. I had so wanted to fearlessly take on each hill as I had done just a few weeks before, but today was just not the day.

My third run of the day was down Cheshire Cat. I had done this run several times now and was comfortable starting down, even with the tricky spring snow conditions. Cheshire Cat is a long blue/black run, with three steep sections separated by two service roads and ending up with a gentle run-out to the Olympia Express lift.

I cautiously started down the top section. It was slow, and turning was a bit of a challenge, but I was being careful and saw no significant problems getting to the bottom. Then, about fifty feet above the first service road crossing, it happened.

I was making a simple, slow left turn, so my right ski became the outside ski. On each turn, the outside ski always shapes and steers the turn, while the inside ski is supposed to track along in sync. But on this turn, in these conditions, my inside ski did not want to cooperate and did not turn with the outside ski. The snow seemed to grab the ski and hold it in place, allowing my skis to cross. I do not remember for sure which ski crossed over the other, but I think my right ski probably slid under the tip of my left ski, which might explain why my right ski binding released while my left ski binding did not. Regardless, when your skis cross going down a steep hill, it seldom ends well.

Most skiers will tell you that when you fall, it all happens in an instant, and it is hard to recall everything that happens during the fall. It is not like a slow-motion sports video replay, where you can recall everything in vivid detail. As soon as my skis crossed, I was instantly on the ground, trying to assess how much damage I had just done to my right leg.

Here is what I think happened. I know that my right ski binding released but my left did not. I remember I had to manually release my left ski after I stopped tumbling and sliding. During the fall, as my right ski released, and while I began falling forward down the hill, I must have instinctively planted my boot in the snow to help cushion my fall. I remember feeling a quick sharp pain in my ankle as well as in my knee. But what I also remember is that it only felt like I had maybe sprained my ankle and twisted my knee. I did not have a lot of pain after the fall and was joking with some folks who had stopped to help. I think the ski boot played a big role in limiting the damage to my right leg.

After I stopped tumbling, three skiers stopped to see if I needed help. There were two ladies and a middle-aged gentleman. They asked if I wanted them to call the Ski Patrol. My pride said no, but common sense dictated otherwise. I could not even stand up, much less put any weight on my ankle. Skiing the rest of the way down the mountain was out of the question. So, the two ladies stayed with me while their friend skied down to the emergency phone that was conveniently located a few hundred feet down the hill on the Village Way service road.

Ski Patrol

First on the scene from the Ski Patrol was a young man who demonstrated a level of professionalism far beyond his youthful appearance.

"Hi, I'm Eli," he said. "Tell me what happened. Where does it hurt? Did you hit your head? Were you ever unconscious?" Those and other questions, as well as his actions on the slope, left me with a positive impression of the Winter Park Ski Patrol program.

Junior Ski Patrol member, Eli

Soon to join us on the mountain was Randy, who would skillfully pull me in the sled down to the Ski Patrol office for further evaluation. Although Randy was the senior Ski Patrol leader on the scene, Eli skillfully directed the rescue operation while also coaching a small group of junior Ski Patrol trainees. They carefully splinted my leg and helped me onto the sled before Randy took over and hauled me down the mountain.

I must have made a comment about how young Eli looked, because Randy assured me that he had all the skills, training, and experience required of all Ski Patrol members. The only thing he was not allowed to do at his age was bring an injured skier down the mountain on the sled.

The ride down the mountain was smooth and uneventful. I occasionally raised my head to look around. I knew the mountain well enough to know where I was, and although I knew that some of the slopes we went down were steep, Randy provided a safe and comfortable ride to the Ski Patrol office.

Once inside the triage room, Randy had some paperwork to fill out. How did you fall? Did your ski bindings release? Did you hurt anywhere else? After he finished the paperwork, he had to get my ski boot off. I asked him not to cut my pants or damage my boot, because they were expensive. Not that they were special, over-priced, top-of-the-line ski boots or high-end designer pants. They were just typical Nordica boots and Spyder pants. But ski boots and pants, and all ski equipment for that matter, are expensive; much more so than, say, a pair of jeans and some hiking shoes. They had several years of good service remaining and I wanted them left intact, if possible.

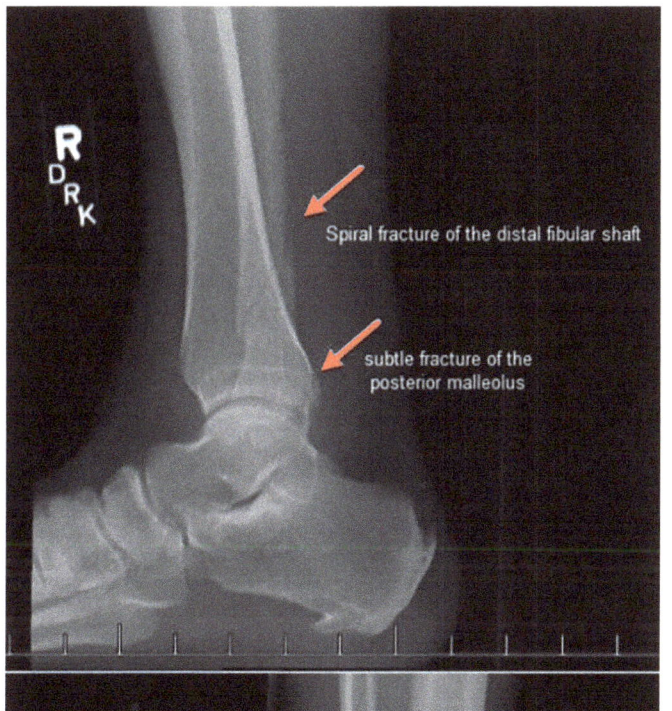

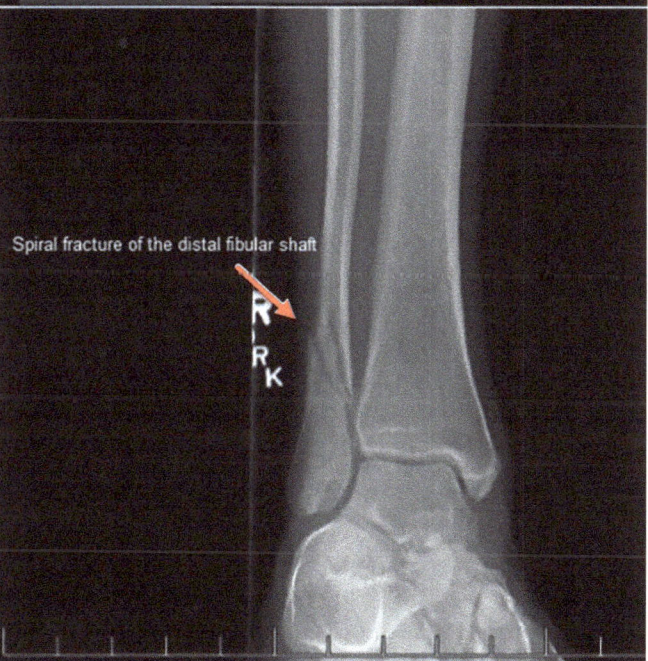

He was able get my boot off without too much difficulty and then asked me if I could put any weight on my leg. I could not. So, Denver Health ER took over and admitted me for further evaluation, again.

After a few x-rays, the doctor told me that I had broken my ankle in two places. I knew that I had injured my ankle, but I really thought I had only sprained it. I was surprised that it was broken because it simply did not hurt that much, except when I tried to put any weight on it.

They were ready to put a boot on my broken ankle and release me, until I reminded them that my knee also hurt. As a precaution, they decided to take another x-ray. More surprises. I had also fractured my fibula just below the knee. It was like a green-stick fracture, where the bone did not break all the way through, but painful, nonetheless.

From the ER, I texted Pam, who was now my boss, to tell her that I would probably be working from home for a while. She once told me that if I ever broke my leg skiing, and could not drive home, do not call her for a ride. At the time she was joking, but I did not know that. So, when she asked why I needed to work from home, I had to tell her I had just broken my leg in three places while skiing at Winter Park.

She texted back with a simple, "Okay." That was all. Just, "Okay."

A few minutes later, she texted again, "You're joking, right?"

No, I was not joking. It was for real.

I only had to work from home for three days and was able to get back to the office on Thursday. Pam lives a few miles from me, and we had been doing our part to save the planet for years by carpooling to work. Now she graciously offered to become my transportation for the next eight weeks if I needed it.

Season Ending

By this time, I was quite sure that my season was over. I began thinking about how much fun I had this season and how much I had improved. It was a full and rewarding season, and I certainly got my money's worth from my season pass. I also began thinking about my other immediate problem. Since I came up here by myself, how was I going to get home? How I was going to get my Blazer home as well, since I had injured my right leg and could not drive? About the only option I had was to call Becky and her husband, who lived in Canyon City. After explaining my predicament, they said of course they would make the three-hour drive up to Winter Park to get me and the Blazer back home.

My day started at 6:00 in the morning, getting on the mountain and skiing around 9:30. My fall happened around 11:00, and I finally got back home around 7:00 in the evening. A long but memorable day at Winter Park, to be sure.

I was able to see a doctor at Panorama Orthopedics on Monday. Dr. Desai looked at the x-rays from Winter Park and put me in a boot for my broken ankle. And for the upper leg, he added a knee brace. He told me no weight-bearing until my next visit. And the pain that I did not experience on Saturday came back with a vengeance on Sunday and the days following. Thank goodness they gave me a supply of hydrocodone.

Three weeks after my fall, I had my next doctor visit and more x-rays. I was hoping they would tell me everything was healing well and that I could ditch the crutches and begin walking with the boot. Instead, I got more bad news. The x-ray equipment at Panorama provided higher quality images and revealed that I also suffered a hairline fracture of the tibial plateau.

A quick search on the Internet confirmed what Dr. Desai told me. This is a serious injury. One more fracture in addition to the others. One really bad day on the slopes, for sure. And, obviously, I did not get to drive home that day.

So, no weight bearing for three more weeks. That was three more weeks hobbling around on crutches. And the knee brace that I stopped wearing because it was irritating? Dr. Desai said to start wearing it again. Ugh.

TAKING INVENTORY AND LOOKING FORWARD

As my fourth season came to a very abrupt end, this story has come to its end as well. While I am sitting in my office gazing out the window, still nursing my broken leg, spring is exploding under another crystal-blue Colorado sky. Just one more reason why we love living here.

Many of the ski resorts are now closed for the season or will be closing soon, and it is time to look forward to warm-weather activities. It is also a good time to reflect on this incredible journey. From my first day four years ago, when I could barely stand on a pair of skis without falling, until now, where I am an advanced intermediate skier, comfortably going down any blue and some black runs, I am still amazed how far I have come, especially for an old man. I have made great improvements each year, although I still have more I can work on. There have also been some setbacks along the way that I need to carefully consider.

In these four years, I have had six significant ski-related injuries. None have curbed my love of this newfound sport, although each should have made me have second thoughts.

On my first day, I rubbed my shins raw at Copper Mountain, costing me eight visits to the wound care center. Then in April, I tore my MCL at Loveland, which ended my first season.

After my first season, I built my own ski machine to save money but then broke four ribs after falling off it. In the long run, I do not think I saved any money after all.

Early in my second season, I fell on the training hill at Loveland, hitting my head hard, and probably sustaining a concussion. I have video to prove that I eventually skied to the bottom of the short hill, but I only remember waking up in the Ski Patrol triage room. I am glad I always wear a helmet, or I might not be writing this story.

Later in my second year, I fell on a blue run at Winter Park and suffered a very painful Type III shoulder separation.

Finally, this year at Winter Park, I broke my ankle and leg, and probably tore my MCL, abruptly ending my season. This one was the most severe injury and will give me a lot to think about during the off-season, as well as a lot of time in rehab.

My friends have suggested that I am just a finely tuned accident, always looking for the next great opportunity, and that I should seriously consider investing in bubble-wrap.

Yet even with these injuries, and the well-deserved ribbing from friends and family, I still enjoy this sport. In the future, I think I will have to be more cautious, especially when conditions are beyond my abilities. I will probably not go skiing by myself anymore, either. I will try to remember that I am not a young kid anymore. That is proving hard to do in other areas of my life as well. But I am still not ready to trade my skis in for a rocking chair.

Compared to that first day four years ago, I think I have come a very long way, especially since I began skiing at an older age. I joked about sharing the bunny hill with little kids, but that is exactly what happened. I do not laugh at anyone learning to ski in their first season. Four years after that first day, I am an advanced intermediate skier, skiing with good form down any blue run on the mountain. I think next year will be even greater than this year has been. I can now focus on more specific areas to really improve my skill, and I hope to take my skiing to the next level. I want to work on skiing in bumpy or cruddy conditions, practice skiing in powder, and try to improve skiing in challenging weather condition with lower visibility. I wanted to try some jumps and learning to ski backward, but maybe those skills will be put on the back burner. But no matter what I decide about throttling back, next year will be another adventure, hopefully with lots of video to show.

I know some will say that four years is plenty of time to learn how to become a fast, aggressive skier. I cannot speak to that. The fast and aggressive skiers and snowboarders I see are all much younger than me, and they look like they have been doing it for many years. Maybe if I had started when I was young, I would have been a better skier after four years. But I will never know. I think that starting this late in life meant, among other things, that my learning curve was slower, and I was more cautious than a teenager or someone in their early twenties. I do not consider myself frail or feeble at all. But with age comes wisdom, and I know what it is like to fall at high speeds. I have had my share of motorcycle mishaps, falls, and other accidents through the years. At my age, I know that when I fall, I bruise, dent, and break more easily, and it takes longer to recover. So, I will be happy to ski at my ability and improve my skills at my pace. In my mind, I am young, fast, and aggressive on the slopes, but my videos often tell a different story.

It is an Addiction

Now that I have been skiing for a few years, I sometimes wonder what the big attraction of this sport is. Do not get me wrong; I have grown to love skiing over the past four years. It is never boring at all. But almost every time we go skiing, I-70 is bumper-to-bumper for many miles, and the slopes are always crowded with skiers and snowboarders of all ages, abilities, and experience. I see little kids fearlessly going down steep slopes in their wide pizza stances. I see young folks, seasoned seniors, and everyone in between, thoroughly enjoying the crisp, cold air and clear blue skies, just for the thrill of gliding down the snowpack at whatever speed their experience allows them.

So what draws us back, year after year, to an activity that is simply riding a chair to the top of a hill and then coming back down on a pair of skis or a snowboard, only to do it over and over again, day after day, year after year? I think it is an addiction. I think that the altitude, weather, atmosphere, and friends combine to release specific hormones and endorphins to cause a permanent, mind-altering addiction that is so strong, it cannot be broken, even over the long, hot summer months during the off-season. In fact, this addiction only seems to be strengthened by those scorching hot days of summer. I too have acquired this addiction. And each year, I anxiously await my first fix around Thanksgiving. Thank goodness there is no cure.

I do not know how many years I have left to ski. I am sixty-four now, and I know that eventually, I will have to give it up, or at least slow down. I see lots of older folks on the mountain, many who are probably in their seventies, but everyone is different. If I have ten years left, I will be thrilled. I wish I could have started skiing twenty years ago. I feel like I have many years to make up, and as long as I stay healthy, I see no reason to quit anytime soon.

EPILOGUE: JANUARY 2019

It has been nearly two years since breaking my leg on the Cheshire Cat run at Winter Park. I had several months of extensive rehab, and my ankle remained stiff and swollen for about a year due to significant ligament damage. But I am completely healed now, with no lingering effects. I did not ski much during my fifth season, mainly because I had no one to go with. And the few times I did go, I was understandably cautious. Maybe too much so. But I did check off another run on my skiing bucket list. On my last skiing day of the season, I did the long and steep blue/black Hughes run, finishing out on Norwegian, a short but steep black diamond run.

But now I am in my sixth season, and I have already been to Winter Park five times. I connected online with another skier, who has been skiing for thirty years. We have gone up several times now, and he has challenged me to go well beyond where I left off two years ago. I can now ski faster with greater control and confidence, and the season is still young. I can also isolate and work on areas where I still need improvement, even while flying comfortably down steep runs. And the areas I am working on are no longer basic skiing skills, but rather refinements to advanced skills. This is where I want to be. Skiing is truly a fun sport now.

Earlier, I mentioned that Cranmer was the hill for me to beat after my shoulder separation. Each time I go down that hill, I can point to the very spot where I fell with such painful results. But Cranmer is no longer the intimidating challenge that it was earlier in my career. For me, Cranmer is now an easy, almost boring run.

Today, Cheshire Cat is my new hill to beat. This year, I have gone back to Cheshire Cat and confidently beat it six or seven times. But each time I go down this run, I still note the spot where my fourth season ended so abruptly. I respect these hills, with the inherent dangers of going fast down their steep inclines. But I am no longer intimidated by them.

To view this video on www.YouTube.com,
paste this link into your browser address bar
https://www.youtube.com/watch?v=LFZhUyi9O-A

To view all my skiing videos, follow this link:
Charlie Avera Channel—Downhill Skiing
https://www.youtube.com/playlist?list=PL42I36FieRrYQQDtHsakdRr-7bFngJsdV
All my ski videos are taken with my GoPro Hero3+ and GoPro Hero 5 Black cameras using a GoPro helmet mount.